Praise

Life in Transition
"Just when you think you've fallen apart, this book will show you how to reinvent yourself by taking ownership of the event, understanding the part you played, and guiding you back to a place of happiness and wholeness."

—Terry Cole-Whittaker, author of
What You Think of Me Is None of My Business

The Intuitive Heart of Romance
"This is must-read for anyone seeking a deeper look into love and romance. Using her right-on guide, anyone can have the relationships of their dreams and bring freshness and passion into their current love life."

—Terry Cole-Whittaker, author of
What You Think of Me Is None of My Business

Tune Him In, Turn Him On
"A powerful aid to a woman's sense of herself in relationship to men."

—Marianne Williamson, *New York Times*
bestselling author of *The Age of Miracles*

"I love this book! Every woman should read it, young or senior. Reading this book years ago would have made relationships a lot easier."

—Terry Cole-Whittaker, author of
What You Think of Me Is None of My Business

"Lively and funny, and based on the premise that women need to take control of their relationships, this is a terrific book."

—*New Age Retailer*

Life
in
Transition

About the Author

Servet Hasan (California) was born into a psychically gifted family in Pakistan. A student of the mystic masters of the Far East, Hasan helps inspire others to attain their full potential through her television and radio appearances, live seminars, workshops, articles, and books.

To Write the Author

If you wish to contact the author or would like more information about this book, please write to the author in care of Llewellyn Worldwide, and we will forward your request. Both the author and publisher appreciate hearing from you and learning of your enjoyment of this book and how it has helped you. Llewellyn Worldwide cannot guarantee that every letter written to the author can be answered, but all will be forwarded. Please write to:

Servet Hasan
⁒ Llewellyn Worldwide
2143 Wooddale Drive
Woodbury, MN 55125-2989

Please enclose a self-addressed stamped envelope for reply,
or $1.00 to cover costs. If outside the USA, enclose
an international postal reply coupon.

Servet Hasan

Life
in
Transition

An
Intuitive Path
to New Beginnings

Llewellyn Publications
Woodbury, Minnesota

FIRST EDITION
First Printing, 2014

Book design by Bob Gaul
Cover design by Lisa Novak
Cover images: iStockphoto.com/11113748, 19466665/Heidi Kalyani;
          iStockphoto.com/18069535, 14198113/Jasmina
Editing by Laura Graves
Interior images: iStockphoto.com/11113748, 19466665/Heidi Kalyani

Llewellyn Publications is a registered trademark of Llewellyn Worldwide Ltd.

Library of Congress Cataloging-in-Publication Data
Hasan, Servet.
Life in transition: an intuitive path to new beginnings/Servet Hasan.
—First Edition.
     pages cm
  Includes bibliographical references.
  ISBN 978-0-7387-3833-8
1. Intuition. 2. Loss (Psychology) 3. Self-acceptance. I. Title.
  BF315.5.H375 2014
  153.4'4—dc23
                              2013037364

Llewellyn Publications
A Division of Llewellyn Worldwide Ltd.
2143 Wooddale Drive
Woodbury, MN 55125-2989
www.llewellyn.com

Printed in the United States of America

Nothing is secure but life,
transition, the energizing spirit.

Ralph Waldo Emerson

With Gratitude

To my father, who named me Sarvat (the legal spelling of my name), which means "treasure" in Arabic, because he didn't bury me alive, as was customary for many a baby girl born in Pakistan at the time of my birth. You are still my hero. And to my mother who not only brought me into this world, but showed me what to do once I got here. Your spiritual gifts light up my life every day. I love you both beyond words.

To my daughter, Sabrina, who has taught me so much more than I could ever teach her. You are not only beautiful, but brilliant. I am proud and honored to be your mother. There are no more words, except to keep telling you how much I love you.

To Terry Cole-Whittaker who continually sprinkles me with invaluable support and encouragement. I love your fairy dust. You sweeten my existence with your unlimited and unconditional love.

To Llewellyn Worldwide for taking a chance on me once again. You opened the door, and I will walk through.

Finally, to everyone who ever broke my heart, I thank you from the bottom of mine. Within every tear that fell, a magical gift emerged. Without you, I would never have become the woman I am.

Contents

Part Two: Healing in the Moment

Exercises

Chapter One

Chapter Two

Chapter Three

Chapter Four

Chapter Five

Chapter Six

Chapter Seven

Chapter Eight

Chapter Nine

Prologue

The only thing the woman wanted to do was end her life. On lunch break from a job she detested but endured, she wandered around aimlessly, not searching for a place to run to, but a place to run from. For although she was an intelligent woman, she was also a self-professed chicken at heart, and couldn't imagine anything as horrifically painful as ending a life, even if it was her own. The distress was like air. She couldn't see it or hold it in her hands, but it was there, always there.

The man she loved for so many years had died unexpectedly, and she was devastated. She felt as if somehow the ground beneath her feet was no longer solid or even real. It kept moving, pulling her down, as if she might be drowning in oceans of fear and rivers of self-doubt.

Nothing made sense. He not only left her alone, but he left her with nothing else, no financial or emotional security. Nothing. There were many strings in the net that formed her demise, but when this one broke, the entire fabric of her existence unraveled.

She crossed the busy intersection, secretly wishing that a car might hit her. One honked and stopped to allow her time to reach the curb. Then, as if to add insult to this nonexistent injury, a man standing outside of a shop smiled and said, "Lucky for you. Maybe you should come inside?"

She glanced up at the marquee above the door. "Run for Cover" was the name of the tiny establishment, a used bookstore. She shrugged, mumbled a profanity beneath her breath, and went inside. Why not, she thought, perhaps she would find a book on how to do herself in with relative ease.

The store was packed with stacks of books everywhere, mountains of literary works, old and new. It smelled musky and damp but was ripe with words of wisdom. The aisles were so narrow she had to struggle to get out of her own way. She stopped, deciding that, at this point, that might just be impossible. Randomly, she picked up a black leather-bound book. There was no title on the spine or the front cover, only gold gilded pages that made it seem as if there might be a treasure hidden inside.

Slowly, she opened the book and started reading. It began with an old fable.

———

Darkness came to God one day and announced, "A major injustice has been taking place!"

"And what might that be?" God asked.

"This Sun of yours is haunting me," Darkness explained. "I have had enough. He is chasing me constantly. I can never get any rest. Wherever I go, there he is, ready and waiting. I have no choice but to run away again. This is ridiculous! You must do something."

"Why is the Sun chasing you?" God inquired, somewhat surprised.

"That's just it," Darkness explained. "I've never once done anything to him that would deserve this kind of treatment. I don't understand it at all. The only thing left is for you to make sure that justice is done."

"Very well," God said, for Darkness had a point that surely needed to rectified.

So God called the Sun and asked, "Why is it that you do this to Darkness? Day after day you chase this poor woman. What has she done to you?"

The Sun was astonished. "I have no idea what you are talking about! This is the first I have ever heard of this. I don't even know this woman named Darkness. And how could I harm her if I don't even know her? I tell you what, you bring her to me, and I will speak with her. I will take care of it. That is all that I can do."

God agreed. But thousands and thousands and thousands of years have passed since then and the case is still pending.

God could never bring justice to Darkness, for God could never bring Darkness before the Sun. They will never meet or know each other, for they cannot exist together. Where the Sun is, Darkness cannot be; where Darkness is, the Sun cannot be.

———

What a lovely story, the woman thought. She closed the book and left the shop. Then she went back to work, to the job she despised. But something shifted within the deepest, darkest recesses of her soul. She did not kill herself, nor did she contemplate doing so ever again. Instead, she turned toward the light and departed upon a spiritual journey that would last a lifetime. No matter how hard it seemed at times, she never looked back toward the darkness again. And almost two decades later, the woman turned out to be me.

Introduction:
The Courage to Change

My heart skipped with joy. For months I walked on a cloud and danced on the moon. I was in love. But then in one split second, everything changed. I turned too quickly, and tripped right over my dreams.

I had lived through the death of my beloved, and although it took many years, I finally met the man I wanted to marry. At least I thought he was until I discovered that the life we had built together was nothing more than a lie. Suddenly my world came crashing down around me, and once again I would have to say goodbye to someone I couldn't fathom living without.

The wounds appeared instantly, splintering my psyche and scraping my soul. Tears of blood filled my eyes. Then they spilled all over my heart, leaving me in a puddle of disbelief. I woke up crying uncontrollably. Completely broken, I wondered if I would ever find the strength to rise up and heal myself as I had done in the past. But I couldn't do that. For once I tried, I realized that the woman I once was had long since disappeared. True, I had lived through the agonizing despair of grief, but this was a new challenge, a new transition. Again I would have to be made anew. I wrote in my journal that day:

Darkness descended,
Night fell.
I cried until the sun rose,
Mourning, again.

Love lived and love died. And I was still alive. I had no idea what to do next.

"Take hold of yourself," the small, still voice inside of me said. "You may have forgotten about me, but I haven't forgotten about you."

There was a long pause, followed by, "Oh, and by the way, stop whining. Get up off your pretty little ass and do something!"

That sounded sincerely full of crap to me. (I never thought I had a pretty little ass.) Really?

I didn't move, of course. It's hard to wake up from a nightmare when you realize you're not sleeping. I was paralyzed by a sense of worthlessness and fear. I lay in bed writhing with anxiety, obsessing over everything I had said and done that ended my relationship. Intuitively, I knew the relationship had been dying a slow and cruel death, at least on my part. I had ignored the situation. I struggled to ignore it the way a woman hears contempt in a lover's voice and struggles to misread it. You *know*, but you don't know. You *don't* know, but you know. The truth gnaws at you; it grows inside of you like a slowly growing tumor.

The undercurrent of fear had been swirling around my gut for months, yet I chose to disregard it completely. How could I, of all people, do that? I had written books about listening to the whispers of our souls and following the path of our inner guides. I used it to find a new relationship in *Tune Him In, Turn Him On*, and again in how to nurture the bond of love in *The Intuitive Heart of Romance*, yet I had no clue what to do when I ended the relationship with that man. It's funny how everything I taught suddenly went out the window when it came to a failed love.

Just as I felt I wanted to die, the universe was trying to tell me to do just that. It could not make me into someone new until I did. To experience a shift in consciousness that would create real and therefore lasting change, I would have to become someone different. Not just when it came to relationships, but in all areas of my life. I would have to examine the moment—or the two or three or ten—when I fell into an old pattern of fear and self-loathing. I felt haunted by these mistakes, and I didn't want to become lost and bitter and say things like, "Love sucks. Why get involved in something that always ends?"

"Get over it already," doesn't work either. Wouldn't that be nice? It's almost as simple as denial, isn't it? And, because I have been schooled in spirituality from Eastern philosophies, I automatically bypassed the general "advice" I received, most of which revolved around retaliation, anger, and revenge. To me, these common reactions would only lead to more helplessness and despair. I wanted to delve deeper into the suffering and discover the compassion, understanding, and peace that would create the ultimate transformation. As Dr. Elisabeth Kübler-Ross so aptly put it, "If you truly want to grow as a person and learn, you should realize that the universe has enrolled you in the graduate program of life, called loss."

I had to figure out where *I* went wrong. My only failure would have been to not learn from this experience. That meant I couldn't run away (and trust me, I wanted to). But running away from change is futile. There is no growth without growing pains. Loss creates change, no matter how small or large, and it provides us with the grandest opportunity we will ever have: to learn more about ourselves and to become more self-realized, more self-actualized. Dealing with our transitions may be difficult, but not dealing with them would be far worse.

Obviously, I had to dig deeper. How much of what happened was my fault? I'm going to say all of it, even if it's not true. It's not my place to police the universe and other people's understanding of the lessons they need to learn. I can only deal with my own. And I set out to do just that, hoping my intuition would send me in the direction I needed to go. If I started anywhere it would have to be there. I had to go back to basics and rely upon my own truth, my own inner compass, to guide me through this deeply passionate grief. After all, reading tea leaves and tarot cards, examining the lines on the palms of a hand, observing auras, and delving into peoples' energy fields were common practices for me. I grew up around this phenomena and it seemed as natural to me as watching my mother bake cookies or plant a new garden. I had been preprogrammed with innate psychic ability and I didn't exactly operate in the world the way most people do. My intuition does not simply play a small role in my life—it *is* my life.

The first thing I did was to stop lying to myself. When I did, I found my authentic self, the real me. The real me—and the real you—are naturally intuitive creatures capable of living a life full of pure magic. My gifts manifested as they never had before. I realized that the journey on the path to the perfection of our souls included losses of all sizes and shapes, those that slip through our fingers unnoticed and those heart-wrenching losses that cripple us for many years to come. Either way, the trials and tribulations we face are not meant to punish us, but rather help us learn and improve ourselves. Life was not hard if I followed my inner guide.

Intuition is not something I believe takes years of reading and practice, nor a talent one must jump through metaphysical hoops to obtain, but rather a natural and normal ability anyone can access. That inner wisdom is already a part of your senses, just as attainable as any of your other senses. Even though you can't touch it or see it, you can experience it. And when you do, it opens you up to more of who you already are.

Every challenge we encounter happens when we are not in touch with our own inner wisdom. Instead of expanding my intuition into the solution, I got thrown off-center. I wanted to know why bad things happened; why people hurt each other; why there was loss, pain, suffering, illness, death. Why did people have to be separated from their loved ones?

The truth is that when we obsess over our problems, we become the problem. If we stay centered, we become the solution.

Once I realigned with my inner guide, I realized that total love does not create guilt but honest communication; not with the other person, with ourselves. When our own individuality shines, there is nothing wrong with telling someone not to call anymore, to move out of the house, or file for divorce if it comes to that. I could then embrace my decision, instead of retracing it. I found patience, acceptance, tolerance, forgiveness, and allowance, creating the expansion my spirit needed in order to heal. I didn't discover my weaknesses through this transition... I discovered my strength.

I wrote this book so you could find your strength, too. We will all experience some type of loss; even our intuition cannot prevent this. We are always losing something, even if it's simply time, youth, innocence, or a conviction we once held dear to our hearts. Whether it's the major loss of a loved one or the minor loss of our ideals and beliefs, you cannot—and will not—avoid it. You can deny it, become a victim, crank up the music, and pour yourself another drink, but you can never escape it. We are immersed in a river of loss. But rather than drowning, we can sail down the river toward the gifts that await us when we reach the shore.

This book is for any life traveler who wishes to navigate the journey of their lives through the wisdom of their souls. Together we will wind through the pain and find liberation. We will climb over grief and find solace. We will swim through growth and find true compassion. And at the end of the journey, we will have arrived home, into the center of our being where there is nothing but a love so profound it is beyond comprehension.

In Part I you will realize and claim your loss. By accessing the rich wisdom of the universe available to you through the gift of your intuition, you will begin to awaken your soul. You will naturally open up to owning and dealing with your transitions, exploring karma's role, and experiencing your feelings on a deeper level. You can then understand that there is no such thing as loss, but rather life lessons within each situation. As you deepen and broaden your intuitive skills, you can and will magically move through the first stages of a transition with ease.

Once you've gotten a sense of what loss really is, naming it, and owning it, in Part II you'll learn how to shift your perspective of any challenge you face, be it from someone or something, a financial crisis, or the loss of your own well-being. You will learn how to apply universal principles to your daily life and love who you are right here and right now. In doing so, you will finally be able to forgive yourself and heal.

In Part III you'll find spiritual solutions that guide you across the rocky terrain you have traveled to sacred ground. By taming your "monkey mind," you can live in harmony with who you are, receive the abundant gifts the universe wishes to bestow upon you, and learn to live in the light. This is where you meet your true self. A life in transition will naturally lead you to your true essence by uncovering your essential self, the part of you that can never really hurt anyone or be hurt by them.

The exercises at the end of each chapter include a soothing meditation to expand your reality. By using concepts like aura cleansing, you can clear your energy from the inside out and heal your heart. While opening the chakras, you can surrender your soul and shed your fears and find positive passages that lead you toward your true destiny. Once you are calm and relaxed, you can embark on a guided written exercise. As you journal, you will be directed to the next level of your personal growth process. Lastly, there's a spiritual practice that provides a road map to the next level of consciousness. Every transition we go through leaves behind a wake of past feelings and emotions. These exercises are designed to provide you with a dustpan to sweep them up into and empty along the way.

Life in Transition is not only for those who suffer a loss, but for those who accompany someone else who does. You may take this trip alone or you may hold someone's hand as they explore the process of transitioning their way back to wholeness. Either way, your compassion and integrity will only improve as you go, and neither of you will ever be the same.

I also offer an invitation for you not to intellectualize the book so much as experience it. Absorb each section, and allow it to resonate at your deepest level. If you do, you will find that it will hit you right between the eyes...or I should say right in the middle of your third eye, helping you awake to the gifts that are yet to come. I filled this book with personal stories, anecdotes, practical exercises, reflections, and aphorisms that will allow you to make contact with the dimension of your intuition. By doing so, I could address life's most challenging moments in a practical and accessible way that would work for anyone.

Your own intuition will become the receptor that can pull down the information you need to face your difficulties and create a new beginning. It's not just telling you what to do, but it will show you how to do it—how to actually move through the entire process of literally reinventing yourself. I like to think of it as a handbook for rebuilding your soul.

In writing this book, I learned to be thankful for the challenges I faced, for without them there would have been no awakening. The difficulties I faced actually created the energy necessary for the flowering of my consciousness to the next level.

As George Eliot said, "It is never too late to be what you might have been." I discovered she was right. I seized the grand opportunity to live the life I really wanted to live. Instead of crawling into a hole, I came into the sunlight and found heaven. Through this book, it is my humblest desire that you experience the same miracle within yourself.

Part One

❧─────❧

Realizing
Your Loss

Monday:
Drowning in loss.

Tuesday:
Drowning in doubt.

Wednesday:
Drowning in despair.

Thursday:
Drowning in helplessness.

Friday:
Drowning in fear.

Saturday:
Drowning.

Sunday:
Just drowning.

One

Beginning
the Journey
Through Loss

I once came across a story about the Buddha. A woman visited him after her child passed away. She was devastated, and begged and pleaded with him to bring her child back to life. He said he would help her if she could bring him back a mustard seed from a home that had not suffered from death. Elated, the woman set out upon a journey that would take her far and wide for many, many months. But she couldn't find a home that had not been affected by loss. Finally, she returned to him and admitted her failure. She could not find one family that had not been touched by death in one manner or another. With this, she finally found solace.

How many moments of our lives are marked by loss? A child gets sick, we discover one of our parents has cancer, a spouse loses a job, you lose your job, the mortgage can't be paid and the house is going into foreclosure, your best friend moves to another country, your child leaves for college, car repairs deplete your savings account, your uncle is diagnosed with Alzheimer's. The bottom line is this: aging is inevitable, every career will end one day, and every relationship is temporary.

There are obvious losses, such as death, divorce, a catastrophic injury, loss of money or a job. And there are also not so obvious losses such as the loss of a dream, waiting for the results of a medical test or a lawsuit, and putting your house up for sale. These are just a few examples, but suffice it to say that loss affects everyone—the good, the bad, and everyone in between. It does not choose sides. It does not play favorites. It is a fact of life.

One definition of loss is any experience that destroys a sense of what we feel makes our lives normal. My definition is that loss is the destruction of expectations. In either case, the anguished cries of plans gone awry will force you to create a new life, one in which you are required to grow and change and to let go of what no longer serves you. We create what we want through a series of life's ups and downs. So, for every down we have, it will inevitably be followed by an up. The good news (and there is good news), is that if you recognize and follow your intuitive yearnings, you will find a renewing gift buried within every challenge you face.

On more than one occasion in my life, autumn arrived with a blistering chill. The vibrant leaves that had once decorated my life with majestic colors turned brown and died. I could not stop this any more than I could stop winter from riding on autumn's coattails. It's a natural part of life, as natural as the sweet scent of the promise of spring in the air and the bountiful summer that ensues.

Not only do the seasons change outside of us, they change inside of us as well. What I could do was choose to focus on the tiny green sprouts that would eventually poke through the frozen ground in the spring. The only way I could do this was by holding on to the direction I received from my eternal compass that would undoubtedly guide me toward the next stage of my spiritual development. After all, the only person that would be with me throughout my entire life would be me. No one else can really direct you, as the answers you seek are inside of you, and you alone.

Many of us are uncomfortable about the transitions we face. When things go wrong, we are sometimes surprised to discover that we feel almost embarrassed, as though we had something to be ashamed of. This is because most of us are taught at a very young age that we are supposed to win, and having challenges may be considered some sort of failure. But even winners lose something along the way in life.

When I started writing this book, I sat down to name a few of my losses. What have I really lost? I've lost plenty of men, including one to death, which made me lose hope and a belief in love. And, later when I was blindsided in a relationship, I lost the capacity to trust. But I've also lost my innocence, opportunities, time, money, patience, energy, friends, family members, not to mention two dogs who were my best friends. I've lost the ability to run a marathon. I've lost a home. I've lost lunches I wanted to share with old friends, a photo album with pictures I cherished, and a ring that meant a lot to me. And, on more than one occasion in my life, I've lost track of my purpose.

But as I shined a flashlight over all of these losses, it occurred to me how much I gained along the way. I learned how to love more deeply; to appreciate and be grateful for all of the people in my life, successes, and monetary gains. I have learned to embrace all of my mistakes and to love life. I learned that when one thing ends, something else always begins—something better.

No matter what we have gone through or continue to go through, all the incidents will help us uncover the gifts we have inside of us, gifts that will provide the tools we require for a greater life experience.

Your intuition may not be able to prevent a bad break-up, stop an employer from laying you off, or prevent a child's terminal illness, but it can help you discover how to grow and move past these types of events. All of us have the innate ability to look, see, hear, and feel beyond what we understand on an external level. We are able to delve into the realms of the infinite that resides deep within us. Our sixth sense makes us strong and capable and aware. Intuitively, we will find that even if we must cry, there is a good reason for it, and someone will be there to wipe away the tears.

There is an old Sufi saying, "When the heart grieves for what is lost, the spirit rejoices over what is left." The universe doesn't give us a problem without also providing the solution. If we want to become who we truly want to be, our challenges are meant for our benefit, even if it may not appear that way at the time.

The moment that makes you feel as if you can't go on is telling you to do just that: It is driving you to confront every issue you have ever avoided facing and find the essential truth about who you really are, whether you like it or not. Remember, the truth shall set you free, but it usually gets you pretty riled up first! However, if you don't face the issues you conveniently swept into the hidden recesses of your psyche, they will keep returning. Perhaps you knew all along they belonged to you, these things you didn't want to face, but you kept putting them off and putting them off, until finally something happened that forced you to face them. The universe wanted you to heal.

Change is going to happen, no matter what. If you want to have a different life experience when it does, then you have to do something different, and *be* something different. In this way, you embrace the change, and find the wisdom that lies within.

You will find, as I did, that there is magic inside each and every one of us. You have amazing abilities that you haven't even considered. You've already been given the gift of intuition that will chauffeur you toward the right choices and decisions. When you discover this, you find power from the inside out. You will drop your pretenses, shed your fears, embrace who you are, and find heaven on earth. And it all comes from understanding the inexorable dance between gift and giving, giving and gift. They are one and the same.

Dealing with Loss

Have you ever found yourself hitting the roof when something minor goes wrong? Have you ever found yourself wanting to go back and yell and scream at your boss after you got fired? Have you overreacted when a loved one didn't call, stood you up for a dinner date, or suddenly isn't as available as they used to be? Don't most of us wonder how we will cope with our feelings of failure after a divorce?

Okay, be honest, am I the only one who has had these disparaging thoughts blasting around in their brains? I don't think so, because I'm not the only one who has allowed a minor loss to call up all the gathered energy of a major loss from the past. If loss is not dealt with, it accumulates over time.

Nothing eludes our psyche. Our subconscious stores all the information over time until something happens to trigger the outpouring of all those pent-up feelings.

It should come as no surprise, then, that we cry our eyes out over a minor disappointment.

If you are facing a challenging time in your life, you simply cannot afford to ignore it. Sooner or later, the remnants of the difficulty you faced will rear its ugly head and bite you from behind. There's a story about a woman who had a recurring nightmare about a monster chasing her. Every night the monster grew bigger and bigger and more and more menacing. For days, she woke up in a cold sweat, crying and shaking. Finally, she had had enough and that night when the monster chased her, she stopped and turned around to face him. "Why are you chasing me like this?" she asked the beast. "I don't know, lady," the monster replied. "It's your dream."

The point of this is that dealing with your transitions may not be easy, but running away from them doesn't work. We cannot afford to forget to listen to the guidance, which we all have readily available to us that will get us back on track.

Your intuitive nudges may come in a form of a dream, as it did with the cooperative monster. Or you may receive images and pictures. Albert Einstein was a great believer in intuition. He once said that many of the elements of his creative solutions came to him through visual images. You may experience a feeling or emotion. In the second *Star Wars* movie, *The Empire Strikes Back*, Luke Skywalker asks Yoda, "How am I to know the good from the bad?" Yoda replies, "You will know through peace and calm." Yoda was telling Luke to trust his intuition.

Your body may also play an important role. Most of us have experienced a gut feeling or butterflies in our stomach. The Japanese even have a special word for it, *haragei*, which means "stomach art." Some people get goose bumps, chills, or their hair may actually stand on end. It doesn't matter how it comes to you, only that it comes and that you pay attention when it does. This is how you receive the guidance you will need to finally move forward in the right direction.

Why Me?

Everyone I know who has faced a challenging transition will eventually find themselves asking why. "Why has this happened to me? What did I do to deserve this? Why am I in so much pain? Why didn't I do something differently? Why didn't I see it coming?" Sound familiar?

Unfortunately, this type of thinking does nothing but drain your positive energy, which makes you feel bad and keeps you stuck in a cycle of sadness and depression.

Perhaps, the best example is from the Book of Job in the Bible. To summarize, Job worshipped God faithfully and had a loving and prosperous family, but Satan believed that Job worshipped God only because of the status and comfort he had achieved. In order to test this theory, Satan caused Job to lose all that mattered to him: his family, his wealth, even his health. In the end, Job did not renounce his spirituality by cursing God, but asked, "Why?" The answer Job was given—in fact the answer that we all seem to find at some point—is that the answers to all of our "whys" are not as important as what we decide to do with our lives and our spiritual potential. The Book of Job suggests that the world is not fair, that immense tragedy and loss can find us at any moment, sometimes for no good reason. Living a just, spiritual life does not exempt you or anyone from suffering. Instead, it prepares you for the inevitability of change.

Questions are bound to arise when there seems to be no explanation for the dark night of our souls. This is where your inner guidance will be invaluable as there are no universal answers, only personal ones. Through your intuition you will find what you seek on your own terms. Even if someone else has been through what you have been through (which, trust me, people have), their answer will not be your answer. Likewise, even if *you* have suffered from a similar challenge in the past, this one will be unique in and of itself. You cannot generalize a situation or a relationship. All you can do is allow your intuitive compass to point you toward new avenues that have yet to be explored.

Well-meaning people will say that everything happens for a reason, or that we shouldn't even question such events. When someone has passed on, sometimes people say that the person is in a better place. When I heard these things after the love of my life died, I frankly wanted to hit them.

If this happens to you, ignore the remark and move to a place of stillness within instead. Say to yourself, "I want to see this situation in a new way. Maybe I can't see the good at this very moment, but I believe I'll come to understand it one day." We are all spiritual beings, sent to earth for the purpose of finding "soul-utions" in a mortal, imperfect world, in which the word "fair" doesn't really apply.

The answers to the riddle of your suffering, why you are experiencing it, what will get you through it, and how you will grow from it are all within you. They may unfold immediately or over time, but if you trust in your inner self, the answers will come.

Understanding Karma's Role

There is only one unique law of karma on earth: cause and effect. Sounds simple, doesn't it? As most of us know, however, it can be a bitch. The truth is that it is far more complex than a bumper sticker or an offhand, misogynist joke.

Karma itself is a word that comes from Sanskrit, one of the oldest languages in the world. Quite literally, it means "action"—in and of itself neither good nor bad. But here's the catch: We are not only living with our own personal karma, but also the karma of every person with whom we interact. And sometimes it may not even be people we know personally.

The karma of individuals interacts with collective karma, which interacts with the karma of the universe. Thus, some will suffer seemingly undeservedly, because of the actions of humanity and because no matter how good any one person is, he or she cannot live life fully insulated from the actions of others or the universe at large.

Let's say a woman is watching a story on the evening news about a man who murdered his wife. Suddenly, she is so distraught by this unknown man's actions that she drops the jar of spaghetti sauce she is holding in her hands and glass shatters all over the kitchen floor. The phone rings, and the caller identification announces that it is the man she has been trying to break up with. Intuitively, she doesn't trust him, yet she can't seem to leave him. Now she's even more upset and doesn't look where she is going…and steps on a piece of glass, gashing her foot wide open. She rushes to the hospital, where she receives stitches from a doctor she instantly finds attractive. He asks her out, and later they get married. In this situation, whose karma is whose?

After having studied just about every religion and human potential movement out there, I have come to the conclusion that they all agree that one of the true purposes of our lives is to know oneself. So in the end, the only karma we can be concerned with is our own. Any type of transition, therefore, should impel us to look inside ourselves. Think about it: Where else can we go? If pain is present, all we can do is go within, find our own inner wisdom, our own divine guidance.

As it says in the Tao Te Ching: "The master does his/her best and then lets go." Whatever happens, happens. The inexplicable law of karma is that every cause has an effect. We must accept our karma and do whatever we can to work with it.

Again, this sounds so simple, yet one of life's hardest lessons is that we can't always control what happens. We think everything is running smoothly when suddenly, wham, out of the blue, the universe says, "Oh, you're looking pretty good. Here, take that!" We get blindsided, sometimes for something we are personally responsible for, and sometimes for what appears to be for no reason at all. Often people are so devastated that they fall into "When Bad Things Happen to Good People" syndrome.

Pythagoras said, "The world is a series of changes, sometimes in your favor and sometimes against you. When you are in charge, do good; when you are overruled, bear it."

In South Asia, there are many tales about Birbal, an advisor to a great Mughal emperor, Akbar, who lived about five hundred years ago. Birbal was considered the wisest man in the land, and was also known for his quick wit. To test Birbal's wisdom, the emperor Akbar asked Birbal, "What words can you give me that will always provide me with counsel, in times of feast and famine, in times of wealth and poverty, and in times of happiness and sorrow? What wisdom do you have for me that will never fail me, and stand the test of time forever?"

Birbal replied, with a smile on his lips, "Your Highness must always remember that this too shall pass."

When we are tossed about between pleasure and pain, we must remind ourselves that nothing stays the same. Being aware of impermanence will help you weather the storms of change throughout your entire life. When you are experiencing something pleasurable, you will experience it with greater presence if you know that this pleasure is also fleeting. At the same time, remembering Birbal's advice can also help you navigate through difficult times. It will give you hope and endurance when things are not going well. I used to experience this when I ran marathons. I could push myself, because I knew there was an end in sight. Nothing lasts forever.

When we assume that our suffering will never end— because so far, it hasn't—we can also fall into what psychologists refer to as "black-and-white thinking." Things and situations as either good or bad. In this case, we are usually peering into the dark side. If we begin to believe our negative thoughts, we then create our future based upon how we view life in that moment. If we feel life sucks and it can't possibly get any better, it won't.

Take a look around, and you'll see that everyone has been hurt in one way or another. Okay, so if that's the bad news, what's the good news? The good news is that it isn't your fault. No one is about to punish you for what you are going through. And even if they intentionally do so, that path is theirs and they will suffer the consequences. They set upon this journey on their own, and they will finish it that way, too. It sounds kind of strange, but if you think of it this way, you really can't take it personally. Combined with the fact that no matter how depressed, battered, and beaten you may feel, your own inner guidance will eventually move you beyond the pain and deposit you safely on the other side. That's your karma—knowing that this too shall pass. Your heart may burn, but you can allow the light of the flames to guide you onto a new and beautiful path.

We don't get a karmic get-out-of-jail-free card for "Oh yeah, I thought that, but I didn't really mean it." The subconscious mind hears everything and simply reflects it back to us. Intuitively, we must be aware that there is no filter to omit what we didn't mean. We are never really going to completely wipe out the memory of our most turbulent times, and we probably shouldn't. We don't want to become unconscious zombies bereft of meaningful memories and feelings. But we do want to find peace, harmony, and acceptance within our own lives.

This is not always easy to do because our human instincts dictate we crave stability and permanence. We feel our most uncomfortable and intense emotions as a result of life's unpredictability. Predictability makes us feel secure, and in turn gives us an illusory sense of control over the ever-changing landscape of our lives. However, life continues to be unpredictable as it has always been. None of us can do anything about it except follow our inner guidance which knows that if and when we leap, there will always be a net beneath us.

Acknowledging Loss

I have a client who recently lost a job as an executive with a large firm. I could tell he was trying to be positive and make light of it. He kept saying it was a good thing, and that he had already received calls from two other companies. That may have been true, but I knew intuitively that he was angry and hurt. Once I allowed him to admit it, he was shocked by how comforting and reassuring it was to openly share his feelings of having been wrongfully terminated. At some point we have to acknowledge what happened to us so we can deal with it and move through it. As long as you tell yourself you shouldn't feel this way or pretend you don't hurt, the loss stays with you. Acknowledging the depth of his loss and talking about it was a turning point in his healing process.

When challenges arise in our life, the biggest one of all will be to stay honest about how we feel. We don't want to lose our capacity to feel; we don't want to become so hardened and frozen that we can't experience or remember the negative things that happened to us. Recognizing our losses keeps us conscious of them until they can be healed. It helps us appropriately process our lives and stay in touch with our own inner core.

I used to tell clients that at some point they had to accept what happened to them, as I thought it was one of the most important steps one had to take toward recovery. I changed my mind when one woman screamed back at me, "I don't care what you tell me, I refuse to accept it!" I realized that for a lot of people, acceptance was synonymous with approval.

Susan did not approve of her loss when the stock market crashed and she lost her life's savings.

Brian did not approve of his loss when his wife had a stroke and became physically challenged.

John did not approve of his loss when his wife was killed by a drunk driver.

Madeline did not approve when she discovered she had terminal cancer.

When I thought about this, I came to the conclusion that they didn't have to accept or approve of it; they merely had to acknowledge it. Acknowledging the loss enabled them to then take responsibility not for what happened, but how they felt about it. They could finally intuit and sense that the loss was real and permanent, and that they could move forward. Whether you like it or not, you have to move into new territory and your intuition will be the only guidance system you have. But unless you take the trip, you will remain exactly where you are.

There is wisdom in feeling how you feel. In this way, you become clearer and therefore more in touch with your own truth. You intuitively stop blaming others for your circumstances.

There is nothing easy about saying, "I just got a divorce," "My wife died," or "I just lost my job," but if you tap into your inner self, you will be reminded that this pain is a sign of your progress toward a new life. You won't feel this way forever.

You might be tempted to fall back into denial, and that's normal, but the only path that will lead you to a new life lies through the mere acknowledgment that it does exist.

Experience Your Feelings

Emotions are real entities. They are energy in motion. But—and this is a big but—how you feel right now is not the way you will always feel. After suffering any type of shock, your emotions will run the gamut from sheer panic to anger to depression. Even if what caused your anxiety is something you chose to do, like selling a home, moving to a new city, or filing for divorce, you may feel a moment of sheer euphoria followed by severe depression. Or if it's something that happened out of the blue, like if you had no idea that the breakup was coming, or the mortgage company is now threatening foreclosure, you may feel devastated and betrayed.

Just know that every high will be followed by a low, and every low will be followed by a high. If you feel torn apart, you will be put back together. But if you continue to feel torn apart and consistently and definitely believe that your own inner guide cannot move you through this, you won't. Remember, the way we think causes the way we feel, and the way we feel causes us to attract what comes into our lives.

Also, please don't try to keep what happened to you a secret. The fear of how other people will react to you is almost always worse than reality. The sooner you can be open about the situation, the better. There's something very freeing about letting the cat out of the bag. I wouldn't go around telling the whole world, but there should be someone you can trust that should be privy to the desolate places you have walked through in your heart. Your intuition will be an invaluable guide. It will let you know who should know. This is also how you find out who your friends really are. If some people don't understand, well then, that's their problem, isn't it? If no one comes to mind, then you can always seek professional help.

Everyone has felt lost and abandoned. By opening up, you'll find that you are not the only one who has ever felt the way you are feeling right now. You may think that you are losing your mind. You may wish that you could run away or die. You may be lonelier than you have ever felt in your entire life. When you talk about your challenges, you'll find out the truth; and the truth is that none of that is the truth. It is simply a belief that you created and that doesn't make it real.

Listen to this, and listen carefully: You are perfectly normal! What happened to you has likely happened to many others. In fact, I'll bet you it has. And, most likely, they reacted much the same way you did. You won't feel isolated when you open up about crying uncontrollably, harboring bitter anger, having difficulty sleeping, or being drenched by an overwhelming state of fatigue. One of the things I hear clients say most often after they've suffered through a major challenge is, "You mean other people have felt this way? I thought I was going nuts."

Whenever we spin out of control, it's natural to be a bit dizzy and say and do things that seem strange to you and probably those around you. But it's okay to be a bit weird, because in this case weird is just plain old acceptable. After my best friend passed away, I got in the shower with my pajamas on. I couldn't quite function. It wasn't until I checked in with my internal compass that I realized it was okay to do my laundry and bathe at the same time. I laughed and chalked it up to multitasking.

My intuition told me to say the following affirmations while I navigated my way down the winding path back to wholeness:

———

I will not always feel this way.

I am going to be fine. This cannot and will not destroy me, because I am an eternal spirit that is being divinely guided.

Through the light of love I will make it through this, just as those before me have.

I am not falling apart, I am coming together.

———

Remember, you are not your feelings. You are an eternal being inside a physical body, operating through a mind that may or may not be experiencing what it has decided to be something it defined as negative. You—and you alone—get to determine if that is your truth.

You Are Never Alone

I once knew a woman who wouldn't get a divorce because she had an irregular heartbeat. She was afraid to be alone, especially at night, for fear she might have a heart attack. When she became overanxious, she would suffer from heart palpitations and her husband would take her to the emergency room. This happened once or twice a year. But every time she went to the hospital she was diagnosed with acute stress and, after some observation, was sent home. When I asked her to intuitively go within and find the root of her problem, she realized that she wasn't happy in her marriage and if she were alone, she probably wouldn't be subjected to that stress any longer.

Take some time to reach down to your depths to find the times you felt isolated and alone. Maybe it was after a breakup, or within a new setting, such as a school, or job. Maybe it was being alone in bed at night. Maybe it was just a few minutes ago. No matter how painful, pull those moments back to you now. They are the prerequisite to remembering who you are. Not who you were, but who you are right now. If you note the events and describe your feelings at the time, you'll likely realize how unnecessary it was, or still is.

Every one of us was loved into existence for the express purpose of the expansion of our souls. The source from which we came wanted to know itself better. It wanted to know its capabilities, its weaknesses, and its greatness. So it created different "faces" of itself. Each of us is one of those faces, detached from our source with the full intent that we would always be equal to it.

And we are. However, from the instant we were plucked off the tree, so to speak, we began to feel some sense of separation. And why not? We had been a branch of the Tree of Life, total consciousness, only to find out we're now just a leaf being blown around in the wind. At first we felt abandoned until we remembered that we were, and still are, a part of something much grander than our own selves. We are each like leaves on a tree. We are individualized pieces of the whole. When we remember that, we can never be alone.

If you are still anxious about the possibility of being alone, consult your inner wisdom—ask it how you can construct a good and satisfying life on your own. Ask and listen. I guarantee the information you receive will be more valuable and reliable than what you would receive from someone you draw into your life just for the sake of it. The more you embrace your fears, even for the briefest of moments, the more you grow.

Finding fulfillment is really about acknowledging who you really are, a divine being. If you shift your perception of self, and realize that you are perfectly happy with who and what you are, your angst of needing to be with someone will slowly subside. Knowing that you are never really alone will help you heal from the inside out, as explained in the White Swan meditation on page 37.

So You Want Revenge?

Admit it: "An eye for an eye, a tooth for a tooth" has at one time or another sounded wickedly delicious, hasn't it? But as Gandhi once pointed out, an eye for an eye will eventually make the whole world blind.

Still, we're all human, and part of human nature will temp us to believe that turning the other cheek isn't always the right thing to do. If we're wronged in any way, we almost feel justified to contemplate the idea of payback. Well, think again.

The problem with this is that when we harm someone in any way for any reason, it will only come back to us, for all acts are karmic. If someone has harmed us, rest assured that they will suffer their own consequences. Perhaps they will feel guilty, and if not, likely suffer the negative results of other poor choices and behavior. In the end, it is impossible for them to escape the consequences of their own actions, whether it's now or sometime in the distant future.

I had one client whose husband announced that he was in love with another woman and he wanted a divorce. He packed a bag and moved out of the house that night, leaving most of his belongings behind. The next day, my client decided that she was going to burn all of his things. She put all of his clothes and some other items in a bin on the back porch and lit them on fire. The sparks went wild, licking at a tree that was next to the sliding glass door, which she had left open. Within seconds, flames from the fire caught hold of the drapes inside. By the time the fire department arrived, most of her home had been burned. She had become a victim of her own retribution.

Now, that's not to say that wanting revenge may not be a good thing. Did I really say that? Yes, I did. Because if you are angry and vengeful, it means you have moved beyond the initial stages of recovery. Typically, we progress from shock, disbelief, and denial, into anger, bargaining, and depression. Finally, we move into understanding, acceptance, and moving on. All of the stages are natural and necessary to the healing process. Slowly but surely you are moving up the vibrational ladder toward understanding and acceptance. Keep in mind that while I said wanting revenge may be a good thing, acting upon it is not. Revenge always has a boomerang effect. It will come right back at you with the same force with which you sent it out.

Even if you are contemplating getting back at someone and not acting upon it, you really can't do that for long. Continuously ruminating over retribution only breathes more life into your initial feelings, feeding them with validation, and keeping you more attached to the pain. It's a vicious cycle. When you keep the ordeal alive, you will continue to throw dark shadows upon everyone you meet.

Come on, you say, we all have people we would curse if we knew how: the boss, the coworker, the neighbor whose dog poops on your lawn, your mother-in-law, the list goes on. But the truth here is that if we think we will feel better by causing physical or mental harm to anyone, we will eventually bear the karmic fruit of those actions. Know that poetic justice does exist. They will get their just due.

Move Through It!

There's a spiritual saying that goes something like this:

> It's so high you can't get over it,
> So low you can't get under it,
> So wide you can't get around it,
> You must go in through the door.

Time alone does not heal all wounds. Transitions can happen quickly or slowly, but either way it's not because you sat around and did nothing. You can't get around the pain. And if someone tells me they are trying to get over it, I simply tell them to stop trying and relax. You can't get over it.

If you've just gone through a divorce or are grieving the loss of a loved one or experiencing any other major change in your life, you must first and foremost realize that the person, place, or thing isn't going to magically disappear. Whatever occurred has become an intricate thread within the fabric of your being, even if you never encounter that person, place, or thing again.

Deep within the core of our being where the pain began is where we must go to put ourselves back together again. We ground, we center, and then we can find our way home again. Otherwise, we feel splattered and scattered, as if someone removed a part of our bodies and we can't seem to find it again. No amount of work we do on the surface will make us feel whole again. We can move, change our hair color, name, jobs, or anything, and it might help on a surface level, but it won't help on a core level. That's because we cannot reconstruct a building without rebuilding its foundation.

If you stop trying to dodge the challenges by moving around the experience any way you can, you'll blast straight through the door in the middle and come out on the other side with a brand new life that you will adore.

EXERCISES

Meditation: The White Swan

Before any of the ancient religions existed, the wise masters of India practiced a powerful mantra that was said to hold within it the power to transform negative karma, and reconnect us to our own well-being. The Hamsa (which means "white swan") meditation originated from the ancient Vedic tradition. The mantra is called White Swan because when your breathing is purified, your spirit can soar, much like the wings of a swan, and it can take flight beyond your limiting concepts of self. The Hamsa meditation moves us beyond our negative feelings of the ugly duckling syndrome and reminds us that we are all as pure and graceful as swans.

Ancient teachings say this mantra is a vibration of infinite consciousness that connects us with divine love and powerful energy that flows through the universe, and ultimately through each of us. "Ham" represents and embodies masculine yang energy, while "so" represents feminine yin energy.

Sit or lay comfortably in a meditative position, keeping your back straight. Center yourself in the moment and just relax. Let go of your thoughts, and breathe in and out through your nostrils. Hold your breath for a moment, stay centered, and allow yourself to just be. Now, pay attention to your breathing, the air that comes in and out of your nostrils. Focus your attention on the contact of air just below your nose. This will naturally bring you to a place of total awareness and unconditional acceptance that can reawaken your spirit.

Breathe in and out slowly and intentionally. When the air comes into your lungs, speak the mantra "HAM." When the air goes out of your lungs, speak the mantra "SO." Keep repeating this, either aloud or in your mind, continuously until you can't really tell whether "ham" or "so" is coming first or second. They should become inseparable and fuse into the cosmic energy flow of your own divine nature. Let the sound emerge from within.

Meditation is an intuitive process that can only take place in this present moment in time. During this meditation, try to remain unattached to thoughts of people, places, things, events, and time. If thoughts, sensations, or emotions appear, allow them simply to be there. Do not entertain them. Do not attach yourself to them. Let them drift in and out, and turn your attention back to your breathing and the mantra.

Recite it for at least fifteen minutes every day and you will be astonished by the results. You will notice that your worries and concerns will decrease, and a sense of calmness will begin to envelop you. As you recite the mantra and let go of your thoughts, you will naturally begin to feel more connected to the universe and begin to understand that everything is exactly as it should be. You and the Source of all are one. You will come out of the meditation feeling refreshed, renewed, and released from your doubts and fears. The more you do this meditation, the longer your sense of serenity and wellbeing will last.

Journaling: You Are Not Your Problems

Loss. The word itself is rather depressing. It immediately brings about a sense that something is missing in our lives. Suddenly there is a void we can't really understand or don't really wish to address. It is an emptiness we long to fill.

But sometimes it has nothing to do with what actually happened to us. If we lost a relationship, it could just be that we had a fear of being alone, of being financially independent, or suffering from an emotional pain we believed would never heal. Suddenly we are faced with a problem of some sort. And how do we solve those problems?

First of all, what do you think a problem really is? Every problem we have is really a dream trying to emerge. Write down any problems you think you have in your life. Are they a longing which is causing a problem, or is it from an outside source over which you feel you have no control that has you in a quandary? Now write down why you think you have this dilemma. How did you get this problem? Examine what emotions these so-called problems bring up for you. Make a list of the negative emotions they cause you.

If you're like most people, you struggled with the answers to these questions. I did, until I understood that sometimes I have problems because it's easier to keep them than to solve them or grow beyond them. But here's the thing: There are no problems out there, only inside of you! Really look at what you have written. Are you addicted to any of those feelings? You may not believe that you are, but ask yourself this: if these things were so uncomfortable, why didn't I do something about them? The answer is simple: because they may be bad, but they are not bad enough. Once they reach a higher level of pain within you, it's often easier to keep them around and resist the change than deal with it.

Problems can become addictive because they are safe, secure, and they give you something or someone to blame. Understand that any and all of your problems are caused by a negative belief, which caused a negative emotion, which in turn caused a negative reaction. So if it all came out of a belief, it can all be taken away with a different one.

I've attended hundreds of seminars where the topic of belief came up. Belief causes the emotions that springboard all the events in your life, good and bad. Change your beliefs and change your world. Everyone says, "Yes,

yes." And then they do nothing about it. Yes, they know they should change their beliefs, but they really *don't* know how. No one gets to that part. We will. First, do the following exercise, even if you don't know why.

Write down your BIGGEST problem or challenge. Now write down seven things you feel would fix it. What would it be like to live without this issue in your life? It's simply an old belief that created the problem. Now pick the top three solutions to that problem and act upon them! Don't forget to squeeze as much profit as you can out of your problems. The issues that caused the problems are lessons. Get the lesson, and then let it go. The only way we can really solve any of our problems is to own our own power by accepting our divinity. You are not your problems.

Spiritual Practice: Move Out of Your Comfort Zone
Since you have gone through a major transition in your life, I am certain there is at least one thing you would like to change. Think about it. It doesn't have to be huge or a major change, such as buying a new house, or moving to another city. It can be as simple as getting your hair dyed a different color, taking classes in something you've always been interested in but were afraid to explore, or redecorating your home in completely different colors. If you'd like it to be a major change, that's certainly your prerogative. The only condition I ask is to make certain it takes you out of your comfort zone.

Oh yes, I can hear the excuses already. It's not surprising that most of us resist change. We'd rather sneak around the fear and hide in our comfort zone once again. But this exercise is designed to help you see just how painless it can be and that the payoff is often worth taking the chance to find out. If you can't think of anything—and believe it or not, a lot of people can't—it's time for you to check in with your intuitive side and ask it how it would finish the following: "One day, I am going to _____." Now fill in the blank.

What happens next is often where most of us fail. We don't do it. Whatever you've chosen to do, just do it, even if you don't exactly know how you're going to accomplish what the task is or if you'll do it right.

Even if it seems completely unrealistic, don't discount it. I have seen women in their eighties take up ballet and a corporate attorney sell everything he owned to buy a vineyard. You don't have to go to such extremes, but just think about any fantasies you've had around work, home life, and relationships. Don't worry about how it will happen. If you follow your intuition moment by moment, you will be guided in the right direction. Your higher self will guide you along through your intuitive nudges and dreams. You're going to have to buy the paint if you want the wall to be red, so just get up and take yourself to the store. If you don't like it, you can always change it; for now you just need to get out there and do something you've always been afraid to do before. Once you can make a small change, you'll find that bigger changes are so much easier to handle, because now you know how.

Two

Shifting Perspective

In my late twenties, I decided that I should stop dating. I would get close to a man and pour my heart out, only to have it broken in two. I allowed myself to be vulnerable, disclosing my deepest, darkest secrets, only to have them used against me in the end. I was angry at men for hurting me, but rather than figure out where I had gone wrong, I eliminated the problem all together by crawling into a hole and hiding. That didn't last long.

By thinking that the lesson to be learned was merely that I shouldn't reveal so much, I then tried to go into relationships with two strikes against me: I closed myself off and I was angry. If anger isn't brought into conscious awareness, it has no place to go. It will either attack you or morph into inappropriate unconscious attacks on others. It was a good thing I didn't care if I dated or not, because frankly no one was interested. I didn't even have to open my mouth. Between the coldness and the bitterness, most men went running in the opposite direction.

Relationships are designed to help you awaken to who you really are. Whether it's building your career, raising children, or dealing with your parents or your spouse, this is one of the many ways we learn the lessons we are here to learn. Dealing with a family member's cancer may teach us about courage; a co-worker's disability may teach us about persistence; a divorce may teach us to be more forgiving; knowing a terminally ill person may teach us to be more compassionate. Whatever the case may be, we are here for the sole purpose of our soul's purpose in this classroom we call life.

Everything that happens to us and every situation we find ourselves in represent a lesson that could teach us how to take our next step forward in the actualization of our selfhood. As we move through our challenges, we will also receive inner messages that will heighten our awareness and allow us to grow. To understand life's lessons, it's important to remember who and what we are, and why we're here. Yes, "remember," because intuitively, we *do* know.

Before I could enter into a healthy, loving relationship, I would have to follow my intuitive nudges and break the pattern. My reactions were based upon the past, which really had nothing to do with the present. One thing I know with all certainty is that if you continue to do what you are doing, you will continue to get what you've been getting. I not only had to change how I was thinking, I also had to change how I was feeling.

We can learn through joy or through pain, as this is universal law, but either way, we're going to learn. Every time we own a past issue and stop playing an old game with new players, we make a shift in consciousness. We make a different choice, a choice instigated by our heightened awareness that will have the capacity to change our destiny. It is through our intuition that we ask for this guidance. We then trust what we hear so we know what to choose and how to act accordingly.

There is a metaphor that spiritual teachings are "jewels in rubbish heaps." What that means is that we will often find the most meaningful life lessons when and where we least expect to find them—hidden beneath the surface of our pain and anguish. This is where we can discover our most precious gifts. If we engage intuitively with our grief, we will almost certainly find the jewel of a meaningful existence.

These spiritual jewels may be different for every person, but there is always one common jewel to be found in the rubbish heap of your suffering: nothing lasts forever, and we should not take a single day of life for granted.

There Is No Such Thing as a Victim

Victim (noun): a person who is deceived or cheated, as by his or her own emotions or ignorance, by the dishonesty of others, or by some impersonal agency.

This is one definition of the word I found on an online dictionary. According to this definition, and most others I have come across, being a victim sucks. There is nothing to be gained, except a whole lot of pain. So why do we fall into that trap?

The truth is that when we are victims, we aren't taking responsibility for our own lives, even though we may think we are at the time. We are often looking to others to make those choices for us, but instead they take advantage of us and/or abuse us in the process. Some victims are even aware of this, but their own fear paralyzes them and they can't seem to break the bond.

So really, there are no victims. There are those who choose to play the victim role, but they aren't victims. They have just taken on that persona for a few minutes, or a few lifetimes. It doesn't matter what the victim role is, or the dynamics of the role itself. What matters is that so long as we see ourselves as victims of circumstance, we will never gain the emotional experience of the event, and never move past it.

If you put out thoughtforms of restriction, weakness, manipulation, and lack, then someone who can accommodate you will appear in your life. In this sense, the victim and the aggressor actually have the same energy frequency. They attract each other. As a result, both victim and aggressor can learn a life-altering lesson.

If you feel you were a victim in the past or are one currently, it's time to put aside your guilt and shame. Again, we're not trying to understand how it all happened; we're only interested in knowing that we are no longer at the mercy of happenstance, devoid of choices. At some point you believed you didn't have any and so allowed yourself to be victimized. Great, now what? How do we get ourselves out of it?

You move out of victimhood by using your intuition to raise your frequency. Raising your frequency means stepping out of social consciousness. It means that you no longer allow your own negative thinking to control you. It means you trade in your fear-based vibrations for those of joy, sureness, safety, and abundance. It means you understand that you and you alone are in charge of your life. If you weren't, that would mean someone else was, and that person would be the only one who could change you. But that's simply not true. You can choose to be a victim, or you can choose to learn from it.

Victimization is a pattern that can be broken only when the victim has had enough abuse and is ready to become something other than a target for others who need to feel powerful. If you feel you are a victim in life, or in a relationship, stop doing what everyone else wants. Start telling your truth, even if it feels scary at the time. Stop looking to others to define who you are. Often they are hurting us, because we make it easy for them to do so. Stand up for yourself. When you look inside you will see glimmers of the part of you that knows that you are more powerful than you ever thought imaginable. Listen to those inklings and act upon their guidance. They will tell you exactly how you can get your needs met without being abused in the process.

Intuitively, you already know that it is your birthright to create a life that will make you happy, that will bring you that which you desire, when and where you desire it to be. Your inner guide will raise your frequency and hold your hand as you walk up a spiritual mountain to find the inexplicable freedom you came to earth to experience.

Everything Is Not as It Appears to Be

There's an old Chinese parable about a peasant who had a son. He cherished his son, almost as much as he cherished his other prized possession, a white stallion. But one day, the stallion escaped. The villagers were shocked and went to the peasant to offer their sympathy. But the man would not listen to their remarks about how unlucky he must be and simply said "Maybe it's good, maybe it's bad."

The next day the white stallion returned and behind him was a dozen or more wild stallions. Now the villagers were envious and couldn't stop telling him how lucky he was. Again, the man simply said "Maybe it's good, maybe it's bad."

Shortly afterwards, the son decided that he would try to tame one of the wild horses. But the horse threw him off, and he fell and broke his leg. The villagers returned, and, again they offered their sympathy, telling him once again how unlucky he was. The only thing the man could say was "Maybe it's good, maybe it's bad."

While the peasant's son was recovering from his fall, the army passed through collecting all the healthy young men for battle. Only they did not take the peasant's son, as he was no use to them. The villager's returned with their usual refrain: "You are so lucky!"

The peasant had nothing else to say except "Maybe it's good, maybe it's bad."

————

Sometimes what we think may be a curse can be a blessing in disguise; there are no accidents in life. It may be years before we see the gifts that emerge from our grief, our pain. But in the end, it will make itself known. Maybe it's good, maybe it's bad.

Life Is What You Make It

Any personal ordeal you face is a turning point. The problem is, we often don't want to go right, left, or anywhere else for that matter. We want to stay right where we are and control the situation. But we don't really have control over anything outside of ourselves. And the only way we can control that is through our response to what is happening.

No one makes us feel a certain way, although we are often quick to say "he made me mad," or "that made me sad and depressed." It may well be justified, but we are still responsible for our reaction; the other person is not.

I had a client named Sue who came to me one day and informed me that someone was after her husband. Sue said that this woman had told her friends at a church group that she prayed every day that he would leave Sue and that she visualized being married to him.

"Wow," I said. "What did you do?"

"I listened to you," she answered. "I trusted my intuition and did exactly what it told me to do."

Sue had attended a lecture I had given about a month before on intuition and how it was the doorway through which we can communicate with the Divine. It made me happy to hear that she listened with an open heart. "So what did you do?" I asked again, anxious to know.

"Nothing."

"And … ?"

"Oh," said Sue, offhandedly, "she got my husband. He left me a few weeks ago."

"Really?" I said, somewhat shocked.

"It's okay," she explained. "That woman deserves him!"

Wow, I had to hand it to her. Sue decided she didn't want to be with a man who had a wandering eye and could be tempted by another woman in the first place. Now, wasn't that better than sitting around moping and feeling sorry for herself? You see, it's not so much the cards we are dealt, but what we do with them once they're in our hand.

How was Sue able to turn this around? Well, she intuitively understood that this man wasn't right for her anymore, that he had served his purpose in her life and she was ready to move on.

A client named Evan kept asking himself the same question over and over again, "What was I thinking?"

He had recently been engaged to a woman who left him standing at the altar. He knew about her past relationships and how some of her friends referred to her as the "other runaway bride." Yet he ignored the signs and allowed himself to get caught up in the relationship, only to get dumped in the end. Of course, he wasn't paying attention to his gut feelings, only the romance. But what's most interesting is that it really didn't faze him. He said he could choose to let it get to him or not. In the end, he was glad he hadn't married the woman. "I don't want to be with someone who can't commit to me."

Once both of my clients got clear on what was really going in their relationships, they shifted their perspective. The power of our minds can change the way in which we view anything. No matter the circumstances, we and we alone can alter how we view people with our thoughts and attitudes in ways that will positively transform our own lives.

Life is about choices. When you cut away all of the debris surrounding a situation, what you will uncover is a choice. You choose how you will react to situations, and you choose how you will let people affect you. No, we can't control the events of our life. We gave up that choice when we were born. When my father was diagnosed with cancer, he said to me "I didn't expect this, and there's nothing I can do about it except to choose to be a victim or a survivor. I choose to be a survivor." I'm happy to say that my father went into remission and, at the age of eighty, has been cancer-free for many years. I am convinced that it was his perception that got him through. Exercising our choices keeps us from feeling helpless as we try to cope with life. It is also another way to avoid making a terrible experience even worse.

The next time you are faced with an upsetting circumstance, consciously bring to mind the choices you have in this situation. Acknowledge that your only goal is to find serenity and peace and that you want to resolve the conflict with love and compassion. Then decide which choice is right for you. Listen and trust that the answer will come to you. It may not come immediately. It may arrive later, in a dream, or through a conversation with a friend. Or it may be buried within something you are compelled to read. But the answer will come.

Be Angry, Be Afraid, Be Insecure

I was counseling a woman a few days after she had lost her husband. Intuitively, I could tell that the knowledge that she was gaining inner strength, offered her little, if any, consolation. She openly admitted that she didn't give a flying hoot about how strong she was getting. She insisted that her heart was broken, and she could literally feel it shattering inside her chest. All she could say to me was that she never wanted to be this strong. Why couldn't she just remain weak?

I could understand her frustration. It's a very human emotion, and I wasn't asking that she suppress or repress it, as that doesn't work. No one wants to be broken-hearted. No one wants to go through a divorce, be grievously injured, or face the cold hard truth of a death of a loved one. But it's part of being alive. It's easy to get philosophical until it happens to you. Healing is personal because it's something you do, not something that happens *to* you. In the beginning it's normal to get pissed off and angry. It's one of the stages of grief.

But what she could do was channel those feelings into something much more constructive. The anger she felt inside was merely energy that she could take hold of before it burned her up and destroyed her. When I first met her, the pain she was experiencing was almost a knee-jerk reaction, as opposed to a feeling she could use constructively.

I asked her to intuitively see what would help her redirect that anger. I remember, as a child, that when my mother got upset she would sit and knit or crochet for hours on end. If I received a new sweater within a day or two, I knew something was terribly wrong. As for me, I have a tendency to start cleaning. I'll clean anything and everything until the anger in me subsides and I can deal with it on a more practical level. There are boundless examples of organizations that were built upon someone's incredible loss. We wouldn't have organizations such as MADD (Mothers Against Drunk Driving) if that weren't the case.

By taking her mind off of something that could not be changed, I asked that she intentionally streamline her negativity into some type of constructive action. Awareness is always the truth, and the light will guide anyone to where they need to go.

In the same respect, you may not feel any pain. You may feel numb, probably because you are still in shock. But eventually you will hurt, and when you do, admit it. To feel pain after a loss is normal and natural, it's also a sign that you are human. Although it may frighten you at first, feel it, lean into it. You will find that if you do that it's not bottomless, that it may only be a few inches deep. It is an important part of the healing process that you actually be with the pain. Actually, kind of make friends with it. It may be hard to believe, but when you do this it dissipates its power. If you use your intuitive guidance system you'll find that pain is not hurting you, but healing you.

It's also normal to feel fear. *I'm not going to make it. I will never fall in love again. I will never feel good about anything again.* These are familiar fears, and you can certainly feel them; just don't believe in them.

Don't postpone, deny, or run away from your pain. For a healthy period of time, it's okay to just feel whatever it is you feel. Be with it. And don't hurt me when I tell you this, but try to honor it. Honor it now. Everything else can wait. An emotional wound requires the same treatment as a physical wound. If you had the flu, you'd stay in bed. If you broke your leg, you would allow time for it to heal. Your emotional state is no different. Set time aside to mourn.

I know the power of positive thinking would like us to just magically shift the negative thoughts that are swirling around in your head into ones that affirm your new positive attitude. But we don't want to be delusional. To do this correctly you must first connect with your inner self and understand that the sooner you allow yourself to be with your pain, the sooner you can transform it into peace and serenity.

What you repress will only grow stronger. When you resist mourning anything, you interfere with the mind's natural stages of recovery. And why postpone the inevitable? It will only come back to haunt you later. Grief does not forget where you live, because it lives inside of you.

Embracing Uncertainty

Fear always means the fear of the future, fear of the unknown. To me, that's all it is. All fear originates here. Whether it's the fear of death or being lost, ill, broke, or alone, it's all about the fear of the possibility that you may be any and all of those things sometime soon. But to live life to its fullest, we have to be comfortable with the knowledge that all things work out as they should and we need not worry. You have to accept the insecurity of the unknown. That is the price we pay for the blessing that follows.

Do not let fear guide your decisions, your life. Accept uncertainty, anxiety, and yes, fear, as your cohorts on the path of change. When you rely upon your inner guidance, you will naturally make decisions that make you feel alive with excitement about the unknown, as opposed to making them out of fear and frustration. As Shakespeare said, "Our doubts are traitors, and make us lose the good we oft might win, by fearing to attempt."

If you think you are too weak to go on, it is only your fear speaking to you. That fear will go on to create more fears. Will the universe really guide me through this and protect me from pain? Again the fear is asking for a guarantee, a promise that you'll be all right. Life is not built upon guarantees. In existence, nothing is certain, nothing is ensured, and nothing is ever guaranteed. And you know what? That's a good thing. If you knew exactly what was going to happen to you, then what's the point? The whole thrill of life, the journey on which we embark anew in every second of every day would be pointless...not to mention boring as all hell!

Life is beautiful because it is uncertain. If everything were forced upon you, your life would become a prison of sorts. Imagine you were ordered to be happy all the time; talk about what a drag that would be.

All I can say is that when I truly let go of my fears, the universe took great care of me. If there is a God—and I truly believe there is, although I think of it more as a Force than an anthropomorphic guy in the sky—then the one thing I can say with great certainty is that Force is smarter than I am.

With that said, I have an unwavering commitment to the fact that He/She knows what is better for me. If we are talking God into something, or talking God out of it, then we are trying to do His/Her job. Not only that, but if you really need to manipulate the universe, then what you want really isn't right for you in the first place. If by chance, we make something happen and it doesn't agree with the universal plan, I guarantee it will blow up in your face.

The universe's unwillingness to accept our suggestions is sometimes the best possible evidence of its devotion to your better interests. Buddha once said that sometimes not getting what you want might be the greatest stroke of luck of all.

Be seduced into the adventure of life and you will find the protection you receive will be infinite. Your internal compass will guide you along the path. As you learn to look to it for direction, you will find that fear cannot occupy more room in your head. You are being divinely guided. Whenever fear appears, all it will see is a sign that says "NO VACANCIES."

Will the universe take care of you and protect you if you just allow yourself to let go? Try it! The next time you are faced with fear, say the following affirmations:

The universe loves me.
The universe is always planning what is best for me.
The universe is only asking for my cooperation to co-create with it, not against it.

Follow these three truths. You may not get what you want, but you will get what you need to find Heaven on earth.

Finding the Meaning in It All

When I first read the book *Man's Search for Meaning* by Viktor Frankl, it had affected my life deeply. Dr. Frankl was a remarkable man, a psychotherapist in Vienna when the Nazis came into power. Because he was Jewish, he was sent to a concentration camp. Unlike millions of others, Dr. Frankl was fortunate enough to have survived.

Dr. Frankl was not just lucky. He attributed his survival, in part, to finding reasons for his suffering. Despite the horrors of the death camp with all of its depraved human cruelty, he was still able to try and find the meaning in his life. No matter what that life looked like at the time, he felt he owed himself as much. At times, he tried to reconstruct the manuscript he completed that the Nazis confiscated and destroyed. At other times, he simply tried to find meaning in the beautiful sunsets he witnessed through the rows of barbed wire fences.

At the end of war when he was finally freed from the concentration camp, he realized that we can all endure suffering, but only if we have a reason to do so. There would never be a way for him, or most of us, to understand or reconcile how and why he and others were subjected to such cruelty and injustice, but what he came to understand was how he himself could make it through one day into the next.

Often when you sit and analyze the challenges you face, dissecting them into tiny pieces of who said what, and who did what to whom, you likely won't find the answers you seek. There is seldom an intellectual rationalization for understanding why it happened. Understanding then can only mean how it played out in your life and what effect it will inevitably have on you. It means figuring out how you can take the challenge and integrate that into who you are as a person. It means reconstructing your identity and your world after they have been irrevocably altered. In the end, it has nothing to do with what happened to you in the past, but ultimately how you will take that and use it to create a new future.

Each and every one of us will have to move through our challenges in our own time and in our own way. But you can and will move through it with less effort if you turn inward, follow the guidance of your inner compass, and know that you are in charge of how difficult and how long your growing pains will be.

It may be hard to see this clearly when your whole world has been turned upside down and you feel so out of control. It is, in a way, until you decide you have the power within you to can conquer anything. If you really listen to that small, still voice inside you, you'll hear it telling you that you can overcome anything.

EXERCISES

···

Meditation: Giving Birth to Your Emotions

Get into a comfortable position, either sitting or lying down, as long as your back remains straight. Breathe deeply and relax your body. Feel each and every body part become weightless as if gravity didn't exist, and you were floating in air. Calm your mind and allow your thoughts to drift in and out with the breeze of the air moving around you. Focus on your breath as much as you can. Imagine you are still floating, so much so that now you are moving above your body, able to look down at yourself. Keeping your eyes closed, imagine you can observe yourself.

Let the sorrow and grief you feel come up inside of you. Don't push it back in any way; allow it to fill you up inside. Let it bubble up slowly, not unlike water coming to a boil. The emotions you have buried deep inside of you, be they sad, painful, or joyous, are free to enter into your being. You feel no need to run away or hide from them. You can look at them more clearly now and see that they simply came about to teach you something you desperately needed to learn, and that they have served their purpose. You also know that you had every right to feel sorry for yourself and mourn your loss, but you can now let that part of you go because you don't need it anymore.

You continue to see yourself below, but intuitively know that it is fine for you to leave for a few minutes. You rise up higher and can feel the angels guiding you toward the person, place, or thing that caused you so much sorrow. In this moment, you understand that the pain you felt is no longer needed and you can let it begin to flow out of you. You feel beyond a shadow of a doubt that the angels will show you exactly what you needed to learn and that there is no need to hold onto any anger, resentment, or guilt. Allow your mind to birth these emotions back into the atmosphere. You feel light and free and clear.

When the grief you have blocked is no longer with you, the angels will guide you back to your body on earth, all the way into your consciousness. You know that those who left you have gone on, either here on earth or in another dimension. They are on their own path, and you can continue on with yours. If it isn't a person who hurt you, let the situation go, whatever it is. Slowly open your eyes and know that all is right with your life. You are free.

Journaling: Naming Your Losses

It's important to know exactly what it is you've lost. Quite often it's not what you think it is. For instance, I had a client who had to file bankruptcy. But it wasn't the idea of losing money that had her so depressed. It was her self-confidence that was shattered. She had to face the realization that she had failed and that she might never to be able to make that kind of money again. But once she became cognizant of just how ridiculous the idea was, she laughed because she knew deep within her intuitive self that she would not only make a lot of money again, but probably more than she had before. She was no longer going to let a few bad investments take her down.

It's difficult to stay in touch with our inner life when we are carrying around a lifetime worth of raw losses that haven't been processed. Remember that the first step in recovery is acknowledging what we have been through. Writing about our losses is not about getting stuck in the past. It's not about dredging up the muck. We do, however, want to give any of our orphaned feelings a new home. When we bring them into the light of conscious awareness, we can then close the door and let them live in peace.

Take a few minutes to get centered. Give yourself the gift of time to allow your inner guidance to surface. Breathe in and out through your nose, relax your body, and allow yourself to settle and quiet down. Tune in to your inner self.

Now write down what you think you really lost, why you lost it, and if you have healed from this loss. As matter of fact, ask yourself if you think you ever will. If not, ask yourself why you don't think you would heal.

Start by listing your greatest losses, jotting down whatever comes to mind. There is no right or wrong way to do this. If you can't get deep within it yet, then skim the surface at first and just see what comes up. Don't worry about how you've written it. It doesn't even have to be grammatically correct. You can just write down words and feelings to start.

If you feel you have healed, what lessons have you learned about yourself, and how can you apply them to your daily life? Have you stopped blaming yourself? What can you do to be more accepting and forgiving to yourself? Are you hanging onto the unrealistic fantasies and illusion around the loss? For instance, do you still think your ex may come back to you? These are just a few questions to help you get going. Be inventive and creative, but most importantly, write from your intuitive self, from your heart.

Most of the people I work with are moving through a current loss, while others are still embroiled in the past. Start from wherever you are. You can write about a relationship loss, a lost opportunity, the loss of a dream, or something material. What you should write about will just come up by itself when you begin. The most important losses will naturally stand out. By doing this, you'll likely find that a pattern will emerge.

One client who did this exercise discovered that all of her losses boiled down to the fact that she didn't want to be lonely. She was afraid she would never find love and end up old and alone. Others were beating themselves up over opportunities that they felt they didn't take advantage of and their underlying fear was that they would never have another opportunity to succeed again.

Whatever your loss may be, reflect on what happened. Reflect on your deepest feelings. Another client thought that when she started writing, it would be all about the loss she suffered through a messy divorce that had just ended. But once she started writing, all she could work upon was the death of her father at a very early age. She never dealt with losing him, and it colored her relationships with men for most of her life. Her most important feelings had to do with abandonment, and once she acknowledged it, she could deal with her husband leaving her in a much better manner.

What did you really lose? If you lost your job and you equated the job with your identity, ask yourself who you really are. What you do for a living does not define you as a person. Who you are in a relationship does not define you as a person. And certainly beyond a shadow of a doubt, what you own does not define who you are.

Spiritual Practice: Become a Conscious Observer

It is not our natural state to be negative, that's why when we are, we don't feel good. When we have a negative thought, it creates a negative feeling, which then shoots through our body much like an electrical charge that sends out a magnetic wave. We attract what's in that wave of energy and will continue to do so unless we change how we think and, more importantly, how we feel.

Positive energy is always in a higher frequency. I've heard it said over and over again that if we want to change our world, we must first change our frequency. But how does one do that? We have to use our intuition to wake ourselves up and pay attention to how we think and feel. Feeling positive is much more in tune to your natural state, which is why it feels good. And because it sends out a different magnetic field, we then attract more of what we want to us.

Pick a day, an entire twenty-four-hour period, when you will consciously pay attention to how often you and those around you choose to be negative. It doesn't matter if you are at work, the grocery store, listening to the radio, or watching television; pay attention to how much a negative attitude (externally and internally) is subconsciously affecting you.

Step back and note what is really going. When you do, you'll find that people are not really saying what they mean, and sometimes neither are you. You'll also see you are often getting involved in other people's issues and drama for no reason. Note how frequently negative behavior becomes normal. Take the time to study how peoples' body language matches how they are thinking and feeling. How often are those around you discussing their problems, gossiping, becoming naysayers, or acting victimized or helpless? Can they, or you, accept praise? How do you and those around you react to a positive statement? It may take a bit of practice at first, but keep at it and you'll begin to see the truth. Not just someone else's truth, but your own.

At the end of the day, notice where you intuitively reached for the negative instead of the positive. The more you do this, the more you will start to realize how much you unconsciously attract with your attitude. An attitude is nothing more than a clump of thoughts strung together. Pay attention, and you'll naturally start to change the way you think and feel—and as a result, what you receive.

Three

Letting Go of Holding On

Most of us have heard the expression, "Let go and let God." But what does it mean? Does it mean that we're supposed to step back and not take responsibility for our actions? In the beginning, I thought this was a cop out. The idea that things were out of my control made me anxious. That's because I really thought it meant throwing in the towel and giving up on what I wanted.

Ah, but I've learned a lot, and one thing I've learned is that this isn't what letting go is about at all. It's really about relying upon your inner guidance and trusting in that power to take care of what you can't take care of yourself. To me it means there is a wise, loving, abundant energy that always has our higher good in mind. This built-in guidance system directs you toward what makes you happy, healthy, and whole. You will be guided to make decisions that make you come alive with excitement instead of paralyzed by fear and frustration.

When we let go, we are really releasing all of our insecurities, worries and concerns about the future. The universe doesn't need our help with that. It will work the details out by giving us signs and signals, and by drawing exactly what we need to us when we need it. It will naturally grace each step we take on our journey through life.

In a sense, letting go means that you have to get out of your own way. Many of us can't seem to do that, and the reason we can't is because we become attached to the people, places, things, and events we think we can't live without. If we want to create a real change in our lives, we simply have to change some of the things we are attached to, and we're all attached to *some*thing. The question is: Just how attached are we? How much do we identify with our attachments and feel they are essential? How invested are we in those things which seem so important to us? Can we live without them? We will explore this further in the journaling exercise at the end of this chapter.

Nonattachment does not mean you don't give a damn, nor does it imply there is a lack of caring and commitment. The philosophy behind nonattachment is based in the understanding that holding on too tightly to anything (which you really can't hold onto in the first place) will eventually slip through your fingers and give you a bad case of rope burn. Holding on with a controlling nature—as if any of us are really in control—will cost us our freedom. Therefore, it is in our higher self-interest to let go a little, as appropriate, and enjoy things as they come and go without investing in their longevity.

I know a lot of people who are attached to an outcome. They do things because they want a guaranteed result. But there is no such thing.

Melody Beattie wrote in *The Language of Letting Go*: "When you wonder what is coming, tell yourself the best is coming, the very best life and love have to offer, the best God and His universe have to send. Then open your hands to receive it. It's yours."

Have courage and be kind to yourself as you shed the old skin of things that come and go. Allow the fresh, new you to come out into the air and shine. This is the gift of letting go.

Death Makes Life Happen

I think death is nothing more than a cosmic joke. Really I do. You see, I truly believe that each and every one of us is made of energy. And if that's the case, we can't die. It's a known scientific fact that you can't kill energy.

The body may wither and decay, but that doesn't mean *we* do as well. Our true Self remains untouched and unchanged. To me, death then only becomes a change of frequency, a change of focus, a change of clothing.

In that respect, we simply disconnect from the dimension in which we've been living and reemerge into full nonphysical empowerment. But the point of our being here is to learn to have that same empowerment while we're still in our bodies and not have to wait until we kick the bucket to discover it.

You will never die. I found that idea a bit depressing at first. You mean I'm stuck with myself for all eternity? Well, ah ... yes. That's why I think suicide is only a temporary fix. You'd have to come back to get it right later. You can't kill the life force that you are any more than you can kill consciousness. The body is a temporary hotel in which we stay the night and leave in the morning. It's not permanent. It's not your home. You are so much more than a body or a mind. You are an eternal spirit.

One of the hardest questions I've received came from a ten-year-old girl, who stared at me with her big brown eyes and asked "Where did my daddy go when he died?"

This is the story I told her:

———

One morning a group of ants came up from underground to collect food. It was still early and as they approached a plant they were shocked to see that the leaves were covered in morning dew.

"What the heck is that?" one ant asked.

One ant said, "It comes from the earth."

Another ant said, "No, it comes from the sea."

Pretty soon a ruckus broke out, as the ants took one side or the other. They argued over whether the dew drops came from the sea or from the earth. Only one ant refused to join in. The wise old ant said, "Stop arguing. If you just wait, we will know where this strange substance comes from. Everything always returns to its source. If you throw a rock in the air it will come back to earth."

The ants had no desire to stand around and wait for a sign, and continued arguing. But by and by, the sun rose further in the sky and the dew drops were lifted into the air, rising up to the sun and disappearing before their very eyes.

Everything returns to its source.

If you truly understand that, you will come to know that life and death are one and the same. Life is a temporary state where we have a tendency to forget the source, and death is going back toward it and remembering once again from whence we came. If you have lived your life to its fullest, death can only be the same. Whatever you have felt your life to be will ultimately be revealed in death.

My belief is that when someone leaves their physical body, they consciously or unconsciously choose to do so. On the surface it may appear that they were victims of a natural disaster, violent crime, or a deadly disease. Yet on an ethereal level, I believe we are completely in charge of our own soul's journey. The spirit knew what it was doing, even if the body protested. I started to believe this when I felt it. When I worked with those who were close to passing, I could telepathically feel it. I sensed their willingness to make that choice. They let go internally long before their death manifested outwardly.

If you find that you fear death, you probably fear life as well. You can't get into a relationship with someone if you are always worried about the relationship ending. You can't block your door to all your enemies, as none of your friends will be able to enter either. And you can't enjoy life if you constantly fear death. Even at the highest points in your life, death will always be there. Life and death are constantly juxtaposed, separated by not much more than a veil of consciousness. In the realm of the celestial inhalation and exhalation, the two become one and the same. Together they grant us a glimpse into eternity.

It doesn't matter if you've lost your best friend, (which can also include those with fur or feathers), or if you've lost your lover, mate, or child. They may not be here with us at this time and place, but they are not gone. They are rewoven afresh into the vessels of our hearts, continuing to beat a life-giving presence within us that will follow us on every step of the journey we continue to take. If you really want to touch them, intuitively tune into them. They will let you know that they are with you.

Love Never Dies

He said he would love me forever, but it turned out his forever wasn't as long as mine.

A week after the man I loved passed away, I received a package in the mail from him. He liked to surprise me and often did things like that. It seemed that on a trip to Disneyland with my daughter, I had spotted a watch that I fell in love with. But he gave me *that* look. You know—that squinted, sideways glance that let me know it was a bit out of our budget at the time. Intuitively, I knew I shouldn't push it. Yet unbeknownst to me, he must have gone back to the shop and purchased it when I wasn't looking. A week after he passed away, the watch arrived in the mail along with a note that said he loved me. He signed it "Eternally yours." I cried when I read his last message; it didn't seem fair. Eternal ended.

That same day I picked up a book of poetry from my bookshelf and opened it randomly to a quote that hit me in the head like a two-by-four (don't tell me this has never happened to you). The poem was by Dylan Thomas, "And Death Shall Have No Dominion." The line that struck me first was, "Though lovers be lost, love shall not." It could not have been more appropriate, as it speaks of one of our most profound truths: love cannot die, because love is essentially what we are made of. Tapping into that larger love is what we are striving for as we travel along our spiritual path. Being separated from those we love, temporarily or permanently, invites us to take a fresh and deeper look at the meaning of love itself.

I know a man whose wife left him over a decade ago. He can't let go of that feeling of being betrayed and humiliated. He talks about it daily, almost as if it happened to him yesterday. Letting go of failed relationships and lost love are among the most difficult things that any of us have to cope with in life. It hurts. But the good old days are often an illusion, based mostly on our selective memories about the past. When I asked him to reevaluate his marriage and intuitively let his mind take him back to the core of his issues, it really came down to the fact that his father abandoned his family when he was only two years old, leaving his mother to raise four children by herself.

I think the word *love*, like *truth* and *God*, is almost impossible to define. And yet, who doesn't use the word almost every day? In Western culture it tends to be associated with the idea of romance. Television and movies are all about "finding love," and the characters often pin all their hopes on finding a special someone with whom to share romantic feelings. Without that "special someone" to love who loves us back, we tend to think that love has passed us by. What a load of crap! If you really buy into that, you are limiting your innate capacity for boundless joy and happiness.

Love will inevitably bring you into a relationship, and love will sustain you through the loss it will also inevitably bring. But what it will also do along the way is guide you through the illusions you have about yourself and the other person. From there, both of you can grow and change, embracing new ways of relating. Love brings out your truth and shows you how to hold on, and also how to let go. In love we may find our weaknesses, and we will also find our strengths.

Just because a relationship is declared to be over, is it really so? Whether through death, divorce, or a bad (or for that matter, good) breakup, is that it? In the end, what determines the substantiality of love and its significance in our lives is what lives within our spirit, our souls. And intuitively, we must remember that what lives within our hearts stays there forever. It's ours to keep for however long we choose.

So he left you and moved to Tahiti or divorced you and married a younger woman (or man). Maybe for some unfathomable reason she decided that the relationship just wasn't working anymore, that the two of you had grown apart, and suddenly she couldn't stand the sight of you anymore. Whatever the reason, it really doesn't make any difference. One way or another, it's suddenly over. We can't force someone else—or ourselves—to stay in a relationship that no longer serves both parties. They see a possibility we don't. We see a possibility and they won't. Either way, the conversations end, the kisses grow cold, and the flame that flickered, however briefly, dies.

But in the end, love is truth and the truth remains. What we do with that love is entirely up to us. We don't have to grow bitter or cold, or be left battered and broken. If we reach inside, through our own intuition, we will discover how this transition has shaped us and turned us into even better people. We fear loss because it represents pain and pain represents suffering. Yet, we have changed and matured spiritually by being strengthened by what we once thought would destroy us.

Baby, Come Back

When I had my daughter, I was handed not only a child, but the unmistakable lesson that something in me had to die for that birth to happen. My former life had been blown to smithereens. The very foundation of my being would have to be restructured to include another soul. My spontaneous, carefree life would be forever changed as I now had to care for another being.

The irony is that when she left for college, I mourned the loss of that life. I didn't just mourn her leaving, but the inexorable closeness we created as she grew up. I had plummeted straight into the extraordinary freefall of loss that naturally accompanies parenting a child. What parent hasn't said, "It feels like yesterday and now they're all grown up." That's right. They grow up, and then they leave.

I practiced for my daughter's departure in a dance I had done for decades, but when the time came for her to leave, I tripped over my own two feet and fell flat on my face. I thought about her first sleepover, learning to drive a car, dating, and all the other transitions of her life that I traversed quite nicely. But when she left home, it darn near killed me. I no longer had control. I have since reconciled this, but does that mean I don't worry? I'd be lying if I said I didn't. I've just made peace with it.

One of the hardest parts of letting go of our children is letting go of our expectations for them. Nancy's son was leaving for music school, and all she could say to me and him was, "How do you expect to make a living as a musician? Why can't you be a doctor like me?" It's not so much our children we have to release, as our disappointment when they don't share our interests and passions. If we want our children to grow into their unique selves, sooner or later we will have to cut the apron strings. Listen to your internal voice. It will tell you how to react and how to treat your child. Even if you don't want to let go, you'll be forced to do so in the end.

We are vessels for our children, providing a vortex for them to enter this world. We teach them to the best of our abilities and then, like it or not, the rest is up to them. We can shield them, but even if we shadow them constantly, we can't stop life from happening. Only love, that bottomless love we felt when we first held them in our arms for the first time, can sustain a relationship that will change more radically and rapidly than any other relationship we experience.

Letting Go of Places and Things

Places and things will always come and go, from our favorite teddy bear we dragged around as a child, to an old collection of records that made up the soundtrack of our teenage years. From our first apartment and car, to our first home, and maybe to an even bigger home. The passing of time will make changes in our lives, whether we like it or not. What we once cherished will wear out with age; old things will replaced by new ones. We have no control over that, and we never will. But what we do have control over is what we hold in our hearts. Whatever we keep there has influenced who we've become.

On the surface, most possessions do not seem that impressive, but if they are stuffed full of memories they are priceless to us. If we move into our intuitive center, we will find the true meaning of what we hold dear and can then let these things physically disappear, knowing that the sacredness of the object will remain cherished within us forever.

When my client Rosa lost the watch her mother gave her, she cried for weeks. I suggested that she infuse the watch with gratitude for the time that she had it, remembering how much it comforted her after her mother passed away. Knowing that it served its purpose in her life, Rosa could more easily let it go, leaving her hands open to receive many more sacred gifts in the future.

When Your Well-Being Gets Sick

John described his illness as a roller coaster ride. Any ideas of how well he took care of himself were shattered overnight, and with it, his professional image. John's cancer demanded he look deeper into himself, something he had never really done before. When he looked in the mirror, he didn't even recognize the person he saw. He was scared and angry. It wasn't fair. This wasn't supposed to happen to him. And even with chemotherapy, the odds were stacked against him. He might die. Who was this man? He no longer had control or energy. He needed to be taken care of and felt vulnerable for the first time in his life.

As in John's case, loss of physical well-being can rob you of your identity. Fatal illnesses can even rob you of your future. But if you intuitively reach within, you will find that what you fear the most is often what has the capacity to heal you.

You *have* a body, but you are not a body. You are spirit, and none of us have a guarantee of a determined future. Every day is a gift. Every day is a blessing. As we peer into the dark abyss of an illness, know that what we are looking at is not who we really are. We are not defined by a disease. If we drop our masks and the false illusion that we are self-sufficient, we can allow the astonishing gift of love to enter into our hearts and heal anything.

Loss of Innocence

Loss of innocence usually happens at a young age, but if it doesn't get dealt with, can impact your entire adult life. Usually it's hidden in your subconscious and you must let it out, not just to yourself, but someone else. It doesn't matter if it is a friend, a family member, or a professional of some sort, the point is that you get it out.

First, take some time to intuitively identify the loss that is difficult for you to talk about. Think about what your life would be like if you could tell someone else about it. Now, find someone you trust enough to share your experience.

As I said, you will intuitively know who that person is. Trust your gut and you will be divinely guided. Whoever it is should be someone with whom you can openly discuss your feelings, someone whom you know won't judge you. Ask that person to help you identify any positive outcomes there might be if you could share your experience with other people. How might other people benefit from your experience? It always helps to help someone else.

Aging and the Body

Most of us are not used to stopping to look around. We race through our lives. The clock ticks, and at first we don't pay attention. But eventually it ticks so loudly, we can't hear anything else. Then the clock goes digital and seems to speed up, which only makes us freak out a bit more.

There's a submersion into aging that we can never really prepare ourselves for. But what we can do is insulate ourselves with the gained knowledge and fearlessly face what lies ahead. We can ignore the gray hairs, the blue veins, and diminishing senses and use what spirit gives us in return—a life that emerges out of the ashes of our challenges, like a dazzling phoenix. A larger wisdom gently settles on us that sees beyond our old boundaries. Again, we can be made anew.

Matilda had to resign herself to the reality of moving into an assisted living facility. Although she resisted the idea at first, once there she found some pleasant surprises. She mourned the loss of her home, but she gained social interaction and an exercise program she would never have participated in before. As a result, she became physically healthier than she had ever been before. She cooks, listens to music, and has never been happier.

Aging teaches us how to ultimately let go of all the interior things we've clutched to for so long. You no longer have anything left to lose, and you're not grasping, acquiring, and controlling anything anymore. We no longer deny the shadow part of ourselves, as there is no reason to anymore. We can be completely unattached from who we identified with in our career and other people's expectations. We reach a different level of wholeness that allows us to become as unattached as a child and do whatever we please.

Old age happens from the inside, not the outside. Think about this: If you didn't know how old you were, how old would you be? Listen to the age your inner guidance tells you that you are. That's your real age. The beautiful face that wrinkled is still a beautiful face. You are still the same person. The gray hair is still your hair. They are all a part of a life unfolding. Instead of rejecting the changes, love them.

There is only one difference between youth and age. What is it? Youth looks forward, always to something better. Age looks backward, always to something worse. What happens when we reach middle age? Most of us are taught that we can no longer look forward to greater growth, that all we can hope for is to "survive" as best we can before we spiral downward into old age.

The Fountain of Youth is always ahead of you, *if* you keep moving toward a better tomorrow. Your body is constantly being rebuilt and perfection is still eminent, mentally and physically, every day. Every minute you live is a minute of conception and rebirth. Even winter can become your springtime, if you let it. Watch the glorious colors of a sunset at day's end, the way the sun paints the sky as it arcs its way over the horizon and disappears. As our physical state diminishes, our spiritual state emerges even stronger.

I truly believe we are all eternal beings. If you believe this too, then no one is any younger or older than anyone else. So, you can either be waiting to die or get busy being born.

Loss of Faith

It's not uncommon for me to hear clients who have suffered a loss make statements such as "I lost my faith in God after my spouse died," or "How can God allow such a thing to happen to an innocent child? Why did God take my child from me?" On the other hand, I have also heard people tell me that their faith in God was what got them through a horrendous ordeal. Spiritual beliefs can help you cope with major losses and recover a sense of hope.

If you have been through any type of traumatic event, most of you know by now that God isn't going to show up like Superman and save the day. But what I have found, as have many others, is that while going through the crisis, it is our spiritual faith that can provide us with a sense of love and peace. God, as you know Him, may not take away the circumstances, but He can make them easier to understand and cope with.

Follow your own intuition to determine what you believe. The important thing is that it should be what you believe, and not what people are telling you to believe, or pressuring you to believe. Trust your inner guidance and know that it will provide an avenue for you to get through whatever you face.

Hidden Losses

Not all losses are major, but that doesn't mean they should be ignored. When we avoid the impact of minor losses, we become inadequately prepared for the major ones, which will inevitably occur. If nothing else, paying attention to smaller losses helps us understand loss is part of being alive. Look within yourself to reflect on your response to smaller losses and see how you handled them in the past.

A woman once hit the back of my car with her brand-new Mercedes. Apparently her husband had just bought it for her, and when she stepped out of the car, she was sobbing and screaming, "He's going to kill me!"

I was a bit shaken up, but not hurt by any means. The bumper of my car was badly damaged and ready to fall off any second, but to me that was still pretty minor. This woman continued crying hysterically as we exchanged insurance information. Finally, I said to her, "Look, there a lot of people who have car accidents that never get out of the car alive. This is nothing. I'm sure your husband will forgive you. After all, no one was injured, especially you. How can that make him mad?"

She took a deep breath and finally stopped crying. What got her so worked up over what I considered minor? Well, therein lay the answer. She didn't consider it minor. Her security was threatened, not to mention her pride and sense of control. She assumed that this type of thing shouldn't happen to her. But it happens to all of us.

Our Collective Losses

What happens in the life of a nation is analogous to what happens in the life of an individual. At some point, you will face challenges that will encourage you to make a change. Perhaps you knew for a long time that you needed to fix something but for whatever reason, you didn't. You avoided it, procrastinated, or, worse, looked the other way instead. But sooner or later, your life became unmanageable and the universe kicked in with an event that finally forced you to deal with it. You couldn't hide behind your excuses anymore; something had to be done.

As I write this, the shootings had just occurred at Sandy Hook Elementary School in Newtown, Connecticut. I can't even begin to fathom the unbearable grief this tragedy has caused. The forces of fate have dealt the families an agonizingly painful blow that's unimaginable to me. I cried. The whole country cried. I prayed and the whole country prayed. I can't imagine that all of us didn't embrace those children in our hearts as if they were our own.

I cannot think of anyone who was not touched by this horrendous event. I think what hurts us the most is the unjustness of it all. But we live in an unjust world. Suffering is a universal fact. Everyone has felt pain, certainly some more than others, but as yet, there has not been a single person alive who has lived in a constant state of bliss from the beginning of their life to the end.

This darkness of the soul is a collective depression that I know will force us to make a collective change. For once, we can't avoid it because it's in our own backyard. And, just as we are sometimes challenged to change ourselves, we are now challenged to change the country and, ultimately, the world. We can't avoid wars, whether it's within a nation or someone's home, but what we can do is find the strength to make a lasting change.

So, if you think it doesn't matter who you become, how you grow and transform in the face of the challenges of your own life, you're wrong. Who you become is intricately connected to who we as a nation become. You may not be able to help the whole world, but you can help one person's world—yours. And when you do, the rest of the world will change too. As we come together as one, a gift will appear from within the depths of darkness. And the gift will be you.

Mourning the Loss of Mourning

Let's face it, there are some people, no matter how ready they are, who simply don't want to move on. It usually occurs when the mourning process has gone on for far too long, and they are now in a position where they must mourn the loss of mourning. If we put a voice to their resistance it would sound something like, "If anything else changes, I won't be in control anymore. I am not budging. Why can't I get the new life I want by being who I am right now?"

You and I both know that you can't stay the same and be transformed. You will have to move out of what has become the comfortable discomfort.

Change forces new choices, but change is the first choice. If you refuse to move forward, eventually the universe will provide an avenue out for you. Unfortunately, it usually arrives like a tornado, clearing away anything in its path that has been an obstacle to your growth. Swirling around in the eye of the hurricane will likely be your previous habits and thinking. Put another way, when we have resisted ourselves long enough, the very change we have resisted comes anyway, sometimes in a much more difficult way than if we had been more open to moving on ourselves. Some part of us deep down is screaming for our lives to be more colorful, complete, and fulfilled. The universe is listening and it brings us exactly what we request, even when we don't expect it.

Change creates chaos. Chaos needs a catalyst. And the catalyst is you. You cannot separate two atoms without some form of chaos. It's necessary, but the good news is that it doesn't last long. And the result of chaos is usually an entirely new creation.

Sandra was two days away from her wedding when her fiancé dumped her. She knew deep down inside that it was for the best, but for months she grieved and mourned the loss. All she did was go to work and come home and shut herself inside her house.

Part of why we see change as so difficult is because we are overwhelmed by the whole picture or set of circumstances. I asked Sandra to check in with her intuition on a daily basis and just get herself to the point where she would be open to going out. I suggested she meditate on it and picture herself getting into an elevator, smiling, and going to a restaurant. That's all. She didn't have to worry about meeting someone, or how she would meet someone and whether she would have to date that someone when she met him, and the million other thoughts that were crashing into each other in her brain like a bad traffic accident.

The following Monday, a man joined her on the elevator at work. She smiled. By the time they reached the lobby, he had asked her for her phone number so that he might arrange to take her out to dinner. She accepted. They are still dating.

It's not unusual to keep looking over your shoulder when you are trying to get rid of the past, but you must resist. Just keep looking forward and moving in that direction. Miracles happen when we are open to the possibility of infinite possibilities. Change can carry us to the door of an entirely new life experience, but we have to be willing to walk through that door when it opens.

EXERCISES

Meditation: Creating Joyful Memories

So far, we've talked a lot about negativity. In this meditation, I'd like you to take the time to focus on any and all of the good memories that you have had in your life, both the seemingly insignificant and those that were life changing. Transitions are always good for us in the end and although we can't take bad memories and replace them with those that feel good, what we can do is override the negative ones with those that we forgot made us feel special and beautiful. It could be a child's smile, a puppy dog, or your first love.

All of us have something that turned us into who we are in a joyful way. If you look carefully, you may even find them in the times you felt were more challenging. For instance, I have a client who did this meditation shortly after she lost her home in Hurricane Katrina. Instead of focusing on the horrifying memories, she replaced them with the ones of her family hugging her afterwards, her dog jumping on top of her and knocking her down, and the many friends who came to her aid in her time of need.

Close your eyes and take several deep breaths. Relax your body, allowing all your stress to melt away. Keep breathing in and out until you feel that every cell in your body is working in complete harmony. Surround yourself with a golden light. You are in total control of your mind, body, and soul. You can release any negativity attached to anything that has ever happened to you, for all it did was contribute to making you the strong confident person you are and will become. Relax and continue breathing deeply. Focus only on all the good things that have happened to you. Let go of any self-doubt, worry, depression, and vengeance. Know that for as many bad things that have happened, you have come out on the other side. You are stronger, have more clarity, and can now move into a whole new era in your life.

Hold on to the pleasant memories that make you feel warm and loved inside. Smile and keep smiling as you review all of the good that life has given you. Allow the joyful recollections to wash over you, cleansing any hatred and resentment from your mind, body, and soul.

When you are ready, bring yourself back feeling free of negativity and in full control of your true self.

Journaling: Writing Off Your Attachments

What are your greatest attachments? What can't you live without? Is it a relationship, status, money, sex, a house, good food? I want you to try something. Think about what you are attached to. Make a list. Now pick one of the most important attachments on that list, usually the one at the top, and meditate upon it. Now ask the question: "What would my life be like without this?"

Continue to expand upon the answer. Imagine yourself living a different life than the one you have, perhaps without the house, the job, or whatever you chose. Let it drop away. Write about how it feels. Do you feel lighter, or do you feel as if you might lose your mind? You just might find that things are not as important as you think they are.

Experiment with other attachments. What are the stories about yourself that you are most attached to? Are they even real? What would happen to you if you changed them? Is it really true that you can't live without someone? When a man once said to me that he would die without me, then I told him that maybe he should. I couldn't handle that kind of responsibility.

Go with what your inner guidance directs you to think and feel. As you continue to trust the insight you receive, you will come to understand that this invisible intelligence truly is leading and guiding you toward a more peaceful and harmonious life.

Now take out a loose sheet of paper and list all of the attachments in your life today that you'd like to get rid of or, quite literally, burn up. Especially note the ones that carry emotional attachments in relationships, whether it's with your parents, other family members, a boss, your spouse, it doesn't matter. Leave the past out of the equation for now. Dealing with the present will take care of the past.

When you are done, fold the piece of paper in half twice and burn it. Then take the ashes outside. Let the wisdom of your inner self open your hands for you and let those emotional attachments be carried away with the wind.

Spiritual Practice: Creating a Mandala

Mandalas are an ancient Tibetan Buddhist tradition. A mandala (Sanskrit for "circle") can symbolize many things, from divine realms to images for visualization. The artistic ritual consists of designing an intricate geometric design. Then a team of monks will painstakingly assemble it by arranging colored grains of sand, grain by grain, until the work is completed. Lamas will often present spiritual teachings as the monks work.

Upon completion the monks wait several days, have a ceremonial viewing, and then sweep up the mandala into a pile of jumbled colored sand and release it to a stream of running water. The design dissolves naturally into a mixture of beautifully colored patterns, eventually leaving no trace of whence it came. This profound experience reminds us that the complexity of our lives is really a lesson in impermanence.

The mandala you create is symbolic of the temporary nature of your own experiences. When you intuitively dig into your own soul, you will notice that even your breath can teach you how transitory life is. Each exhale is an ending, which is ultimately followed by a new inhalation, a new beginning. The cycle repeats itself over and over again.

As the Buddha lay dying, he told his disciples, "Everything that has a beginning has an end." What he was really saying is that loss is a universal reality. If we examine our everyday existence, we see that nothing is stagnant and that change is inevitable.

When you create a mandala, it is not necessary to go to the lengths of the monks. Simply go outside into a favorite spot you have in nature. Take a deep breath in, focusing on the inhalation of new beginnings…and the exhalation of endings. Let your surroundings sink in.

Intuitively, let yourself be guided toward things that feel good to you. Gather rocks, seeds, grasses, flowers, twigs, leaves, pine needles, and, yes, sand if it is available. Create a pattern in the dirt, sand, or on a poster board if this is more convenient for you. You don't have to be an artist to do this. You can create an intricate design, or simply allow yourself to place the objects wherever you intuitively feel they should go, allowing the creation to appear spontaneously. Either way, take your time and delight in creating this masterpiece, giving thanks to each of the elements that are contributing to your work of art.

When you feel you have finished your mandala, be grateful and appreciate the fine work you have done. Then let it go. Collect all of the pieces that made up your design and return them to a body of water—a stream, a lake, river, or ocean. It doesn't matter, as long as you have let them all go. As you do, think about what you would like to let go of with it. Open your arms, hands, and heart; release it all back to nature. Know that it was all meant to be and will only serve your higher good.

If you are faced with inclement weather or find yourself homebound, you can accomplish the same thing indoors. More often than not, the monks created their masterpieces with colored grains of sand in their sanctuary surrounded by their sacred belongings. I once had a client who created a magnificent winter solstice mandala in her meditation room using different colored glitter. It sparkled, literally and figuratively. The project took months, and upon completion, after meditating upon it for a few days, she found she still couldn't leave the house. So she gathered up the creation in a jar and released it in the bathtub. Use your imagination along with your intuition, and you'll be amazed by what you can create.

Part Two

Healing in
the Moment

I no longer fight
the ache, the pain.
Instead, I blame
no one and begin again.
This is where love's
true nature abounds,
For when nothing
is sought, all is found.

Four

Ways to Heal Your Wounded Heart

On the morning I woke up and realized that I had to say goodbye to the man I thought I was going to marry, I truly thought my life was over. My head felt as if it weighed a ton, so heavy I could barely lift it off the pillow. I couldn't move. I couldn't even open my swollen eyes. There was a throbbing going on behind them, beating to an irregular rhythm that seemed to say "stay put, stay put" over and over again. It was a steady ache, punctuated by sharp pains. It hurt to think. It's as if the wiring in there had come loose and was rattling around in the back of my brain. I imagined it sounded much like it would if you started up a car and realized someone had left a wrench under the hood.

I felt nauseated. I wasn't sure if I should eat or if doing so would make me sicker. I wondered if I had a hangover, but when I pieced the evening back together, I knew I had been too disoriented and upset to drink. Maybe I had a glass of wine, maybe I didn't. Either way, it wasn't enough to make me *this* sick. What was wrong with me? Was I dying? Yes, the old me was dying and I was having an emotional hangover. I'd been mentally beaten to a pulp by other people, and when they were done, I started on myself. I was down for the count.

The idea that I might actually heal seemed foreign to me. It felt a bit like I was stuck in quicksand, and any move I made, most especially a sudden one, would certainly drag me down further. I think I was hoping that I might be magically plucked out of my old life and plopped down into a new one filled with love and light and security. I was looking for an immediate answer to my prayers. Unfortunately, it usually doesn't happen that way. And it certainly didn't happen to me. I forgot that healing is a process. And I would have to experience that process in my own space and time, gaining my own understanding and realizations.

When I asked my inner guidance how I could heal, it only told me that I should be patient and kind to myself. The answers would all be revealed in due time. From that moment on, a profound change occurred. I stopped fighting my anxiety, my pain. I surrendered. Finally, I was willing to let my intuitive self direct me. Out of nowhere, I was inspired to speak to a friend I hadn't seen in years who had a multitude of ideas that would lead me in a new direction. Then an unexpected opportunity with my work presented itself. All the information I was receiving from my inner guide was slowly but surely shifting my perspective. That was the miracle—those many little ones that put me back on to a clear path.

You Will Survive

Survive. The word seems a bit skeletal to me, even a little deceptive. It's not just about surviving in a clear, linear sense, as much as it is about subjecting yourself to change, to the inevitable ups and downs, fears and feelings, and victories and failures that accompany growth. You do survive, or at least you can, but that happens almost by default, by the simple fact of being present in your own life, of being aware and able to act on the connections you make with your inner guidance system.

That said, no matter what happened to you, you will get better. No doubt about it. The healing process has a beginning, middle, and end. There are the standard processes we will likely move through: shock, denial, numbness, fear, anger, depression, understanding, acceptance, and moving on. They vary, but that's basically the gist of it. All you are required to know is that there is an end. It's not that far off. You will heal. Nature is on your side, and nature is a powerful ally. Remember, if you are alive, you will survive.

This challenge you experienced may have been the worst thing that could ever happen to you, but it is not the end of your life. It's just the end of your life as you knew it. It is the beginning of a new one. If for some reason you feel you won't survive and your grief turns destructive (meaning you want to harm yourself in any way, including not seeing to your basic fundamental needs), depression immobilizes you, or you turn to drugs or alcohol, there is no shame in seeking help. The only shame would be to need help and not get it.

There is an intelligence that flows through us all, animating our world. It has a reason for everything that happens. If it brought you pain, it can just as easily bring you peace. Listen to the whispers of your inner voice, and let them take you where you need to go.

Trigger-Happy

It could be a song on the radio, a picture in a magazine, the hush of a conversation, or the gentle clink of champagne glasses. Whatever it is, it conjures up an ancient set of feelings: an old anger, a deep disquiet, a sudden wish to stand up in the middle of the room and scream your head off. That old anger, hurt, and despair have bubbled up inside you, and you feel as if they're going to erupt all over again.

When I've moved through a challenging time, I often felt as if there was a beast inside of me that woke up and started rattling the cage in my head, dying to be released. It's almost as if the beast was angry because I'd been feeling good. He wanted desperately to shatter all of the restraints, and throw my life back into chaos. The beast was rebelling. I had to figure out what triggered that beast back to life.

Seemingly random events, like driving past a restaurant you used to frequent with a loved one, or minor things, such as a photograph, can set off a cascade of overwhelming emotions. Sometimes you will know months in advance how difficult certain events will be for you. I have a friend who always leaves town for Christmas because she still misses her mother.

These events, random or otherwise, are your emotional triggers. Triggers are cues in our environment that signal our emotions. They release a set response of feelings and thoughts you have buried deep within your subconscious mind. Triggers are the places, events, people, sounds, smells, and images that remind you of your loss and arouse that feeling of sadness. Visiting a particular place, hearing a certain song, seeing a particular picture, viewing a certain website, or talking to certain people might bring it about. Even buying groceries for one less person may trigger an overwhelming sense of sadness.

For most of the people I have worked with, the most potent triggers are those that remind them of activities they used to share and celebrations of their lives together such as anniversaries. You may find it cathartic to take out a calendar and mark down what times of the year might be particularly difficult for you. Highlight important dates, dates that were meaningful, and any places you would go, or things you would do together to commemorate special occasions. It sounds simple, but most people don't think about it until it's too late. If you note the dates ahead of

time, you can approach these milestones with empowerment, understanding the trigger's role in your life and why
it causes you to suffer. It's much better than being blindsided by the intensity of your emotions when that date
comes around.

Many holidays originated as a way for people to honor
natural cycles of death and rebirth. For example, fall holidays often acknowledge death or the end of a harvest, and
spring holidays acknowledge rebirth, regeneration, and the
sowing of seeds. Rather than avoiding triggers of acute
grief, strive to understand the role that these triggers play
in your life. As distressing as these triggers can be, grieving
through these milestones will mark a turning point in the
healing process.

If we choose to hide from our pain, we only lie to ourselves, and the pain will come out somehow. If it is blocked
off or numbed, we will be unaware of why we are feeling
the way we feel and won't grow from it. I have one client,
Sally, who took out her pain on everyone else, particularly
her family. When they pointed it out to her, she realized
that it was being at home that made her feel the saddest
after losing her job. Not having anywhere to go every day
was not easy and she fought it, often taking out her frustration on everyone around her. Instead of acknowledging
this trigger, she had channeled it into hatred of her own
home, driving everyone away. Once she accepted that un-
derneath her angst was a tremendous amount of pain, it
became easier for her to stay home while she looked for a
new job.

If we turn away from our feelings when we are distressed, we risk closing off our hearts to ourselves and to our relationships, like Sally did. What triggered this most for me was self-pity. Nothing brought back pain and hatred and disgust more than feeling sorry for myself. I could feel invisible in a room where only I and my pain existed. I could dwell on my losses, one after another and feel sorrier and sorrier for myself, until pretty soon I was back in that same place in my head and heart that I was when I first suffered. Eventually, though, I stopped going to pity parties.

So you hit a trigger. You can't run from it, at least not for long, but you don't want to dwell on it forever either. The best way to overcome a perceived predicament is not to look for ways to ward it off, but to change your relationship to it. So embrace it. Give it a hug. When you accept your feelings exactly as they are you, defuse them. If you focus on what is making you feel sad, or angry, or depressed, you can then, mindfully, accept those feelings and move past them. If you don't know they are there and they lurk in the back of your mind, they will have a tendency to fester and grow. By being aware, you can lovingly accept them with compassion and know that this too shall pass.

Through our intuition we learn that although we can still experience stress and distress as well as happiness and pleasure, the world keeps going on as it always has. It is your attitude toward it and how you approach your distress that changes. Your intuition will show you that there is nowhere to hide from your thoughts and feelings, so you can finally stop running away from them and accept yourself.

Seek Wise Counsel

I'm going to make this short and sweet. I'm not going to tell you who to talk to. Your intuition will guide you to the right person who can provide you with the support and love you need while moving through a transition.

I will tell you who not to talk to. It is not anyone whose well-meaning advice contains any of the following words: "You should…," "You could…," or "You'd better…" Although the person is probably trying to be supportive and well-meaning, it usually only makes you feel inadequate and guilty.

Have a Good Cry

I know several therapists who have what they refer to as "crying rooms." I never forgot about that, and to this day, I always keep a box of tissues handy during any work I do. In fact, I love it when people cry, because to me, tears are a sign of healing. Crying is actually one of the healthiest things a person can do. Did you know that tears of sadness have a different chemical composition than tears of joy? Tears of sadness release substances that have a calming effect. That's why we often feel better after a good cry. Toxins, both physical and spiritual, are being washed out of your system. Therefore, it's logical to say that if you don't cry you're keeping those toxins within you.

Some men believe they're emasculated if they have a good cry. Though we've come a long way, especially since we can now watch a romantic comedy and see grown men bawling like babies, there are men who still don't feel like they're allowed to open up and have a good wail. That was originally the purpose of the crying rooms. Real men do cry. So, have at it.

Drop Your Baggage Off

I used to be a cleaning freak. My house and everything in it had to be immaculate. But what I was really doing was trying to please everyone else. I was trying desperately to perfect my outward environment, because I couldn't perfect my internal one. Once the man I was living with moved out, it didn't seem so necessary to clean house all the time. By asking him to leave, it seemed I had started to clean my internal environment, too.

Our baggage is usually filled with awful, ugly patterns that have developed out of underlying fears we have not addressed. The first step is to recognize them. Patterns are situations that come up over and over again. Faces may change, even the city may change, but the underlying dynamics at work stem from the same source. They cycle through our lives giving us opportunities to make a different choice. In that way we change our response to a given situation.

Perhaps you've picked up these patterns from your parents or other relationships you never understood or dealt with. Most often they are all subconscious. For instance, I have a client who continually attracts unavailable men. She came to me asking why the same situation kept repeating itself over and over again. She just didn't get it. She was choosing the same men over and over again, men who then gave her the opportunity to choose differently. As soon as you understand your patterns, the universe will register that you get the lesson, and the cycle will stop. And that piece of baggage can get dumped in the trash, where it belongs.

Repetitive issues are the same way. How many times have you found yourself in a situation where you felt someone took advantage of you? Someone borrowed money and didn't pay you back. Someone betrayed you or lied to you. Just when you think you've got it, the same thing happens again. It repeats itself, and now you think you deserve it. No, you don't.

You heal when you intuitively go inside yourself and find the fear that created a lack of self-worth in the first place. Ask yourself why you allowed someone to take advantage of you in the first place? I guarantee that the answer will involve your wanting the person to like you in some way. If you examine this further, you'll undoubtedly see that you needed someone else's approval to feel good about yourself. If you don't figure it out, I can guarantee you that the lesson will repeat itself. The universe is infinitely patient. It will mirror back to you exactly what you are ignoring.

Watch what you say and the actions that follow: "I can't live without a glass of wine before bed" and "I always eat when I am nervous or upset" are programs you have incorporated into your subconscious mind. I know so many clients who developed the pattern of eating to comfort themselves. All of it came down to them beating themselves up in some way because they were disappointed with their lives.

Determining when and how this pattern of feeling helpless and trapped in your body began is not always easy, but once you realize what you're doing—that you are just reacting to patterns that have been coded into your subconscious mind—half the battle has been won. For instance, if you tell lies, ask yourself if it's coming from a fear of being disliked. Perhaps it makes you feel like you're in control? Are you obsessing over your ex because you feel lonely? Are you yelling at your kids because your life didn't turn out the way you wanted it to? Whatever the underlying meaning, your intuitive self will likely take you to the root of the problem, and you will come to understand that it was only your soul trying to help you win this game we call life.

The only way we can change our experiences in life is if we finally step back and look at our habits and patterns objectively. Once we identify repetitive situations that do not serve us, we can ask our inner self how we can react or respond differently the next time it happens. And yes, there *will* be a next time, trust me. But when we are faced with the same predicament in the future, we simply won't entertain it.

Courage is what it takes to face your fears. Using your connection with your inner guide will give you the ammunition you need.

Un-Addict Yourself

Again, if you feel you need professional help, please get it. I am not an expert on the subject, but I do have something to say. (Who would have guessed?) Listen, I've been there. I think just about everyone has. We've all been addicted to something, or worse, someone. It's not uncommon for people to respond to an emotional upheaval by overindulging in one way or another. Whether it takes the form of food, alcohol, or sex, it really doesn't help in the end. All you are doing is covering up your fear. Instead, find someone you can talk to, preferably someone neutral and impartial. What you need is an understanding ear or two, not another donut.

When we abuse any substance, we are only camouflaging what's wrong, perhaps not physically, but mentally. We are searching for a room in our mind, hopefully one that has no windows or doors. We don't want anyone looking inside, and we don't really want to look out at the world either. We want to be transported, taken away where no one can find us, including our true selves.

It's a very real and enormously seductive phenomenon to be able to take psychic flight by ingesting something and leave ourselves behind. Nina wanted to take that flight, and sometimes still does. She recounted how she would drink in order to pour herself, quite literally, into a new personality. She could unstop the bottle, pop the cork, and slide right into someone else's skin. It was a liquid makeover, from the inside out. I saw it on her face. She became someone else when she drank. And she couldn't stop, either. She would go out and see couples huddled together drinking wine by a fire, friends celebrating over champagne, people sharing secrets, solving problems, falling in love. The images crept inside of her and settled into the dark corners of her mind, places where fantasies thrive. But when Nina drank, it melted down the pieces of her that hurt or felt distressed. In that process, space was made for some other self to emerge. A version that was new and improved and decidedly less conflicted. It momentarily solved all of her problems.

It's an equation that goes along with all addictions: discomfort plus whatever you use to drown it out equals no discomfort. As for Nina, she believed she'd really been transformed. She became someone she liked. All the crap she was dealing with at work and in her relationships disappeared.

Some of us wrongfully associate this "second skin" with self-enlightenment, something that turns us into the person we wish to be or the person we think we really are. It makes everything better—that is, until it makes everything worse. You may be lifted and shifted, but you're still who you were. The real you may be trapped inside, locked in a cage beneath your ribs, but sooner or later she will surface. And when that woman does, you may hate yourself for what you've done.

One client did a deadly dance of rolling one addiction into another. She would compulsively overeat, filling her with shame and sexual inferiority, which then gave her self-loathing and doubt, which led her to drink too much, which temporarily countered the self-hatred and filled her with chemical confidence, which led her to sleep with a man she didn't know, which led her circling back to shame and overeating again.

I have a client who every couple of months has a need to go into a discount shop and steal something silly. This is a very wealthy woman we are talking about, but something deep down inside of her needs to feel shameful and bad, so she'll creep into a store and stuff something in her purse. I have another client who will go into just about anyone's medicine cabinet and steal their Valium, Xanax, or whatever she can get her hands on. One woman I know gambles on anything and everything she can find that can take her pain away; pain caused by self-hatred.

At their heart, all addictions are driven by the same impulses. Most accomplish the same goals no matter what path one takes to get there. But if we really want to bypass any kind of addiction, we have to throw the map away.

Kicking addiction is not about willing yourself not to indulge in those behaviors anymore either, because wouldn't that be nice? Instead, it's about becoming the kind of person who doesn't need to do those things anymore, who couldn't even imagine it in their wildest dreams. You may need help with that or you may not. Your inner guide will tell you if you really have a problem. It's up to you to listen and take action if necessary.

One thing I learned the hard way is that what we learn from the hard knocks we receive in life happen with a clear mind. If your mind isn't clear, you don't really get the lesson, and you stay stuck. Dishonesty, secrecy, withholding information, and self-medication are the threads that form the cloak covering your real self.

A woman I know didn't grieve her father's death until almost a decade after he passed away. The false pleasures of remaining numb lulled her into a dream world. She needed to get sober first, and when she did, she finally cried for his life and death, and cried for all the regrets he died with. She cried with a mixture of sadness and wonder and guilt, understanding for the first time that she had been holding on to the pieces of him she cherished: his insight, wisdom, and charm. But she also left him behind in some way, finally giving herself the chance to move forward toward something better.

Hit Delete

The next time you find you are falling into a negative frame of mind, stop yourself. Where did that thought come from? Be an investigative journalist in your mind. Think back to the first time you felt inadequate, stupid, insincere, or rejected, and ask, "What even introduced this emotion into my life?" Do your best to determine why this message stuck with you and why you accepted it as part of your reality.

Now say "Delete!" Instead of continuing with a negative belief, first take yourself away mentally. Think of something pleasant. Your intuition will take you exactly where you need to go. It may be to a quiet secluded spot on a beach where you can watch the waves curl into the shore, or it may be a high on a mountain where you can see eagles fly. Make whatever place you chose your special place. Look at the beautiful view; let the sights and sounds sink in. Become one with the scenery.

Next, take yourself away physically. When negative thoughts come into your mind such as "I'll never find the man of my dreams," "I'm never going to make the kind of money I need," or whatever, do something different. Find something healthy to replace the destructive behavior. One client started knitting in order to help her quit smoking. Another took up running after her sister died from breast cancer so she could participate in charity marathons. Take a walk, do jumping jacks, write in a journal. It doesn't matter what you do. Any diversion will eventually crack a negative pattern if it's done often enough.

What you are doing is breaking the synaptic impulses that keep playing the same record over and over again in your brain. Think of the habit as a computer program. If you didn't like something on your computer screen, you wouldn't sit there and yell at it. You wouldn't demand that it just go away. And, even if you did, we all know nothing would happen. What you would do is hit the delete key. And, once you deleted the negative programming, you would replace it with something that worked.

One more thing: once you've successfully accomplished keeping yourself from a harmful, negative emotional or physical habit, make sure to reward yourself by giving yourself kudos and big pat on the back. We're all born with talents and imperfections that we can learn from, but the shortcomings can be transformed into power once we face our demons. When you admit you have a negative pattern and you take positive action to overcome it, your soul will smile.

Color Yourself Healed

Your moods are colored quite easily. It's no secret that you will likely feel completely different if you walk into a dark room than you would if walking into a bright green or yellow room. Hundreds of studies have been done on this. I'm not going to get into it to that degree, as I could certainly write an entire book on this subject alone. But even if you scratch the surface and use your intuition to guide you, color can and will have a profound effect on you.

Our spirits can be pulled up or down by our surroundings. Try to stick with the spectrum of colors that naturally make you feel good such as red, orange, yellow, and green.

Green can be quite soothing, as it is the color of the heart chakra and promotes healing.

You don't have to redecorate your whole house. Changing your bed sheets to a pastel green can help your heart and soul find growth and healing. Buying some plants can liven up an entire room. Wrapping a bright yellow scarf around your neck can lift your spirits when you're feeling down. An orange pillow can bring a dark corner to life.

Even if you like the colors, avoid black and blue for now—I'm sure you've beaten yourself up enough already.

Go Jump in a Lake

If you are trying to deal with a sick parent while raising a child, are in your midlife years and must make a career change, or are overwhelmed with debt and paralyzed with a fear of the future, it doesn't make any difference—you can still rely upon your inner guidance system to give you the answers. But you have to listen and in order to do that you must find time within the trying times to nurture your soul.

Think about what just came to your mind when you read the words "nurture your soul." What constitutes taking care of yourself? It could be flying a kite, taking an endless walk on a beach, a week's vacation to somewhere you've never been before, or a day at a spa. These are things that we generally think of when we stop and feel we need a break from it all. But what if you could do one thing on a daily basis that would help replenish your soul?

Things are so much easier to handle for us when we find balance, calm, and peace within our everyday lives.

Everything we do is infused with the energy we put into it. If we are internally a mess, then what happens around us usually turns into a mess as well. Your internal state will always determine how life flows around you.

Not only should you take time to reflect and meditate, but also to just have fun. Perhaps you can't get up and just leave town to lay on a beach for a week, but you can find time within the spaces of daily living to relax and breathe in peace and quiet and solitude. It could be as simple as taking a walk on your lunch break, stopping to browse at your favorite book shop after work, or doing anything else you feel would provide nourishment for your heart.

Now, this is when you are going to tell me that I should go jump in a lake, which, by the way, is not such a bad idea since it, too, can be fun! You're going to tell me you simply can't find the time. Well, I have found that those who don't make time for some form of recreation will ultimately be forced to find time for illness.

Lisa was heading for a nervous breakdown. Her entire life revolved around accomplishing more, having more, getting more. After she lost her job as an executive with a prestigious firm, I suggested that it might be easier for her to find another job if she nurtured her inner being. She looked at me as if I'd grown another head. She found a way to argue with whatever I suggested, always coming up with another excuse for why it simply wasn't possible. She didn't have enough money in her saving account to cover more than a couple of months of expenses; her kids had a ton of after-school activities; her mother was sick. I got tired just listening to her.

What I asked Lisa to do was pause long enough to contemplate all the things that were draining her, and all the things that contributed to her lack of energy. Basically, she had to let go of whatever she could that sucked the life out of her and find a way to create more balance. In the end, it had to be about what Lisa thought was most important in her life, not what everyone else wanted her to do for them.

Once Lisa stopped letting her energy leak out all over the place, she felt better. Eventually, she created a routine that felt good to her. She felt as if life was flowing again. She no longer felt tired, cranky, and out of sorts. Her brain stopped working overtime to catch her attention with warning signs of how exhausted she was.

When you let yourself have a little fun, you will have a tendency to discover what is most meaningful to you. Often, we're afraid to ask ourselves that question and usually we're scared of changing because we feel that doing so might be more painful than what we're going through. We opt to stay the same and be miserable rather than face the unknown, which could *possibly* be more miserable. But guess what? Kites were meant to get stuck in trees. That's to be expected, and it's half the fun of flying them in the first place.

Turn inward to your own soul and listen to the wisdom of your intuition. It will tell you when you can say no, and it will show you when you need to give yourself permission for emotional, physical, and spiritual renewal. How long do you want to wait to get yourself back to the good life? Your intuition constantly points to the path that will lead you there. Follow it. Allow yourself time for meditation and prayer and any other activity that makes you feel as if you are pampering yourself and you will begin to heal your mind, body and soul.

In the words of Paramahamsa Yogananda, "by the practice of meditation you will find that you are carrying within your own heart a portable paradise."

Here's how you can make that happen…

Follow Your Joy

No one I know—including myself—can feel joyful one hundred percent of the time. And honestly, anyone who told me they could would likely be lying. Part of being human implies that we need contrast in order to learn and grow. We can learn joyfully as well. That is to say that we may not live in joy all the time, but we can live in joy the majority of the time. If you can intuitively find a tiny piece of joy in every experience you have, you will have mastered the flow of energy. Not only will your life improve immensely, but it will do so immediately. You will be on your way to abundance in all areas of your life if you learn this one simple thing: Be happy!

When you learn to feel the joy of what is in front of you, rather than what is behind you, your vibration will shift to a higher level, the same level as health and freedom, and abundance. How high you vibrate on an energetic level is directly proportionate to how joyful you feel. Is it that simple? You bet it is. The happier you feel, the more attractive you become, and I'm not just talking about your physical self. I'm referring to your energetic Law of Attraction self. That's why when you're in love, you look so good and life just seems fall into place. Well, fall in love with yourself this time! Marvel at what a wonderful person you are. Appreciate everything and everyone around you.

Follow your joy!

Adopt an Attitude of Gratitude

I truly feel that if you can adopt an attitude of gratitude, even the most difficult life circumstances can be considered blessings. Gratitude naturally makes our lives more full. If you are grateful for the simple things in your life, you can feast upon its pleasures.

Your mind can only have one thought at a time. And have you noticed how hard it is to let your inner guidance speak to you when you are angry, frustrated, or depressed? Gratitude is the single most important tool for turning negative thoughts into positive ones.

Start where you are, no matter what your circumstances may be. Enlist your intuition's guidance and allow it to uncover what you can be grateful for. This will naturally create a dynamic shift in your energy flow, redirecting it to a place where new possibilities exist.

Be thankful for what you have right here, right now.

Take Good Care of Yourself

Transitioning is hard work. In some ways, it may turn out to be the hardest work you've ever done. But I can tell you one thing: usually when the healing is hard, the rewards are the greatest. While you are going through a trying time, it's imperative that you remember to take care of yourself. When we go through anything traumatic, our immune system will be compromised. Sleep more, eat well, and exercise if you can.

Intuitively check in with your body and see if there is anything it needs. Do it regularly and often. And listen to it. If you are craving eggs, you may need more protein. If you need to sleep, it may be because your body is fighting off an infection. Your body is an amazing machine, and if you listen to the messages it is transmitting, it will tell you exactly what it needs.

Walk the Path Back to Wholeness

Sometimes we walk through life as if we were in a dream, not really conscious of who and what we really are. The only way we'll have whole lives is if we dwell within the wholeness of our true selves. When we remember that we are one with the source of all things, we'll cease to have nightmares.

It isn't easy giving birth to our spiritual potential. You might think the labor pains will do you in. They won't, though, because it's not a matter of becoming metaphysically complicated. It's the path of simplifying your own internal thinking as you apply certain basic principles to your everyday life. We reprogram ourselves at the deepest levels, and then through the alchemy of the divine curriculum, we'll meet the people we're supposed to meet, in order to go through the situations we need to go through, in order to learn the lessons that will transform us. We have to let go, surrender, and stop trying to be right all the time. We must detach from the opinions of others and rest ourselves in the arms of the here and now.

It's like falling in love with yourself; just as you would relax completely in the arms of a lover, you will completely relax in the arms of the universe. You become comfortable within yourself. The anxiety that keeps you in a constant state of franticness disappears. You begin to feel free of past hurts, able to face life fearlessly once again. A new energy emanates from within you, attracting exactly what you need when you need it.

This is the dawning of a new time in your life. You do not have to postpone your happiness until everything you want is perfectly aligned. Maybe you are waiting for your bills to be paid, for that new person to show up who will sweep you off your feet, or to be offered the job of your dreams. It actually works the other way around. You get what you want when you are happy. So stop waiting and try to be happy. Happiness does not exist out there in the world. It's a choice you make every minute of every day. Even if it's just for one minute at a time, it's better than how you felt before. You have access to the gift of divine intuition to guide you toward those moments.

Hints of Healing

At some point, you'll know you're getting better because the questions you ask yourself will shift and change. Instead of asking yourself why this happened to you, you'll find that you start to ask what you should do next, or you might ask how you can grow from this experience. Either way, what you have done is accepted life's detour, and now you can actively search for the right road that will lead you to the life you want to live.

Divorced people will start to consider dating, someone losing a home will start checking out ads for places to live, someone who has lost a spouse will consider moving, or redecorating their home. However it manifests on the outer plane is inconsequential. Internally, your inner guidance system is moving you out of one consciousness into another, one that will move you forward.

Become Self-Investing

Self-investing is not the same as being selfish. On my last trip out of town, I remember listening to the flight attendant explain to the passengers about the mask that drops out of the ceiling of the plane to provide oxygen in case of an emergency. She also said that if you had a child, to be sure to place the mask on yourself first and then on the child. As a mother, that never made much sense to me. It's a mother's natural instinct to help her baby first. But now I understand: you can't really help anyone else until you help yourself.

EXERCISES

Meditation: Heal Your Heart Chakra

Whenever you have a gut-wrenching feeling, your hair stands on end, or you get a sudden chill down your spine, these are a direct result of your intuitive self awakening a chakra and giving it physical form.

Think of your chakras as satellites stationed in your aura that pick up different energy vibrations. There are seven of these psychic energy centers, located along the spine from the tip of the tailbone to the top of the head. Each chakra vibrates at a certain speed, and they all work together to balance your body.

The only chakra we are going to focus on right now is the fourth chakra, also called the heart chakra, located in your aura at the level of your heart. It is a beautiful emerald green. This chakra vibrates faster than the three lower level chakras, as it is the center of love in your consciousness. We're not talking about romantic love; this chakra controls your self-acceptance and acceptance of others. It also deals with trust, well-being, abundance, prosperity, and good health. It is the point of consciousness where a person can feel the pain and joy and struggle of themselves, others, and even of the world. It is the empathic center. I will often open my heart chakra during a reading because it is the gateway to perceiving another person's experience.

If your fourth chakra is out of whack, you may feel resentful or hateful toward someone or something, even if you think you have forgiven them. You may do things out of obligation rather than a genuine sense of benevolence. You may start to feel isolated and disconnected from people and the world around you.

If your fourth chakra is over-stimulated, you will likely have a tendency to resonate too strongly with other people's emotions. If you are around someone who is depressed, you'll start to feel that way almost instantly. You may start to obsess or worry unnecessarily, causing you to be too controlling, or, on the flip side, codependent.

Sit down comfortably in a chair with your back erect. Breathe deeply. Now imagine that there is a beautiful angel hovering above your head. She's holding an antique jug filled with a healing emerald green light. She tips the jug and pours the light down into your crown chakra. The light melts slowly into your scalp, relaxing your head, your eyes, your nose, your mouth. Drop your jaw. Allow the shimmering emerald green light to flow down the base of your spine, through each and every part of your body. Let it submerge into every blood vessel, every vein and cell. It's moving through your arms, your chest, your heart, your lungs, your stomach, and legs, all the way down to the very tips of your toes. Breathe in and imagine this green light is pulling in waves of healing energy, healing all wounds and hurts and filling you with a sense of love.

Now allow the light to focus completely on the heart chakra. While the light dances about in your chest, place one of your problems or negative conditions into that light. Tell yourself now that you are loved and that the universe provides for all your needs. Everything you do and say will be with love. You are receptive and open to giving and receiving love. Your heart is healing and all your needs are fulfilled. You let go of all resentments. You forgive others and ask forgiveness so that you may lovingly let go of the past. Allow the love of the universe to pour into your heart. Breathe and relax.

Keep breathing, and with every exhale to say, "I am now letting go of all negativity both inside and outside of me." Now allow the green light to center on your heart. In your mind, tell your heart to relax. Keep breathing deeply. Stay in this state for as long as you can, allowing the green light to continue whirling around you.

When you feel ready, slowly bring yourself back into consciousness, feeling energized and better than you have in a long time.

Journaling: Have a Conversation with Grief

Instead of saying "I'm sick and tired of being sick and tired" or anything that you may be saying to yourself at this point, talk to your grief. Here's an example of what one client wrote:

Dear Grief:

I know that you are here for a reason to teach me something. I am open to that, because I really don't want to have to go through this ever again. But it still feels to me like you broke me in two. Sometimes I don't even want to go on. It's tough. Something just keeps telling me to put one foot in front of the other every day. I hope you are gone soon, because I hate this. I hate you. The only thing that keeps me holding on is that I know that someday you will be a distant memory and I can't wait. I can't wait to say goodbye to you.

Anne.

Mourning is a part of the healing process and it is there for a reason, but that doesn't mean you have to be controlled by it. Just when you think that there is nothing left to lose, you will find the first stitches of hope are being sewn into the tapestry of your day-to-day life. If you acknowledge the process, by voicing your side of it, it can bring you back from the edge of despair. Believe that your intuition has the power to help you heal.

Spiritual Practice: Pack Up Your Worries
I have a box on a shelf in my office on which I have written one word: Surrender. Whenever I have a worry or concern I feel is starting to rent out a room in my brain—usually because I am mulling it over endlessly to the point of obsession—I pull down my Surrender box.

First, I take out an index card and I write out whatever my concern might be. I did this exercise with a client recently; here is what she wrote:

I really don't want anything to do with my ex-husband anymore, but he tries to communicate with me every time he drops off or picks up our two boys. I really don't want my kids to see me act badly toward him, so I try to act nice, but he uses this to get to me all the time. I feel stuck. He hurt me so badly, I don't even want to talk to him or be near him. Everything I've tried just hasn't worked. He doesn't get that I need boundaries. I'm surrendering this and asking for some divine guidance here.

After she finished writing this, I asked her to turn the card over and summarize her concern with a question that she would like to get an answer to. She wrote, "How can I get my husband to respect my boundaries?"

Next, I asked that she surround the card with a bubble of white light before she placed it in her Surrender box. She kept her box on her desk, where she could see it often, but rarely ever opened it. She let it go and knew that an answer would come at the right time. It could come in the form of images, or a flash of insight, or words or feelings, but eventually it would come.

Within a week she found the answer. Instead of fighting her ex-husband, she came up with a plan where they would have a weekly dinner with the children together. It didn't get him out of her life, but it seemed to give him what he needed—a sense of unity. After that, he didn't bother her for the rest of the week. It seemed to satisfy them all.

Five

Forgive Yourself

I can almost guarantee that if you have suffered from a loss of any kind, there will be two long-term outcomes. One will be anger, and the other will be a broken relationship. It is as true in relocating as it is with death or divorce, or a change in career. If you've experienced a loss, there is someone you will need to forgive.

Well, now you may say, "What about the other person? Am I not owed an apology? Isn't that person supposed to ask for forgiveness?"

I do hear that a lot, most recently from Shelly, who filed for divorce after she found out that her husband was not only having an affair, but that the other woman was pregnant. It cut to the core of her being, because she had been trying for years to have a baby and never could. Not only that, a year after the divorce she discovered that her ex-husband married the woman and that they are very happy together, while she remained destitute and alone. Yes, he should ask for her forgiveness, but he probably won't. That's not her problem. That's his problem. That's his work. And the only work you can do is your own.

When Jesus, a true master of forgiveness, said "Forgive them, Father, for they know not what they do," he used the Aramaic word *shaw* when he referred to forgiveness. *Shaw* means "to untie." To *forgive* also means "for" (in favor) "giving" (to deliver a gift). When you forgive, you affirm that you are in favor of giving. No, you are not giving someone a gift. Well, that's not true. You are indeed giving a gift, but it is to yourself. You are untying yourself and receiving the blessings of such. When you release another to move along their own path, you free yourself to do the same. Therefore, when you forgive someone, you are giving yourself the gift of freedom. Forgiveness is a gift you give yourself. It allows you to leave the past in the past and move forward.

Shelly was still in pain and felt as if granting forgiveness would make her appear vulnerable and weak. But forgiving her ex-husband was never about him. It was only about her. Forgiveness opened a door, a better door. It allowed her to walk through her grief, disappointment, anger, and pain. She could now get on with her life.

In a way, forgiveness is saying goodbye. There's no right or wrong time to do this. If you have already lost someone or something, saying goodbye is merely recognizing that you cherished the good, and have let go of the bad. You're not dismissing that person, place, or thing from your life. Remember, grief does not end, even though it may stop hurting. It just changes. Whether it's a deceased loved one, the end of a marriage, the places and people we call home, or the body you once had, it needn't be shrouded with sadness. If we dig deeper, we will be guided intuitively to our spirit which knows that everything served a higher purpose.

Forgiveness is not to be confused with forgetting. It does not mean that you are condoning someone's behavior, and letting them off the hook. By forgiving, we are not condoning abusive or negative behavior. It is not a bargaining chip. We cannot forgive someone and trust that they will ever change. They likely will not.

However, when you forgive with compassion, you release the hold that this issue had on your life. Rather than feeling unresolved outrage or a sense of justice not being served, you breathe in the rarefied air of compassion that moves you beyond your ego self into the domain of your higher self. Yuo can then grow emotionally, physically, and spiritually, allowing your wounds to heal.

For your own peace of mind and for the sake of all your future relationships, try and forgive those you feel hurt you. Don't postpone it, for it only delays the healing process. Let that weight fall off your shoulders and the fire in the pit of your stomach finally be extinguished.

If you are still having a hard time forgiving those who wronged you, remember what Oscar Wilde said: "Always forgive your enemies; nothing annoys them as much."

Forgive Who?

If you are not sure if you should forgive someone, tap into your inner wisdom for guidance, and ask yourself the following:

- Who do you feel is responsible for your pain?

- Why do you think they are responsible?

- Are you angry and resentful toward the person? If so, why?

- What part did you play in this situation?

- What happened to you because of this person?

- Can you forgive this person? If so, when?

Hopefully, the answers to these questions will help you unravel the ropes you have tied around your heart. Jessica could not forgive her ex-boyfriend. They dated off and on for ten years, from the time she was forty until she was fifty. He never made a commitment, but what she regretted most was that by the time they broke up for good, she was too old to have children. She blamed him for that and couldn't find it in her heart to forgive him. When she answered the questions above, she realized that she blamed him for her inability to have a child. But really, she blamed herself more than she blamed him. Once she was fully able to understand that she should have left him years before and not stayed in the relationship to start with, she was able to forgive him and herself.

Your intuition, your inner guide, knows exactly how you feel. It's important to dig deeper and ask for instructions. Only by bringing out the true nature of what's happening inside of you can you actually begin to heal.

Say Thank You, Please

If you noticed, in the dedication to this book I thanked everyone who ever broke my heart, from the bottom of mine. Within every tear that fell, a magical gift emerged. Without them, I would never have become the woman I am. I meant it.

Faith plays a big part in this. We have to intuitively trust that every event in our lives bestows a present that longs to be unwrapped and cherished. Within the package are the seeds that have been planted in your psyche. All you have to do is water them and allow them to blossom. When we do, a beautiful flower will emerge, its petals reaching toward the sun.

What did you learn from your now-ended relationship? What was special about your time together? How did your life change within the framework of the circumstances? Perhaps you learned to love more deeply, how to surf, or fix a leaky faucet. The solution to what ails you is in what you took away from it. This is what you thank another for.

Guilty!

What is guilt? It's not just an emotion, but an attitude as well. Usually, it comes about when we feel responsible for not meeting expectations—not just our own, but anyone else's. We feel remorseful for deeds we did and/or didn't do. Guilt can be more damaging than other negative thoughts, as it is usually intertwined with condemnation and remorse, which will keep you stuck in the past.

When people are going through a major transition in their lives, two of the most frequent words I hear are "if only." These two words are the precursor to guilt. And guilt is a worthless energy. *If only I had been there more. If only I had loved him more. If only I had done something differently.* Laying a guilt trip on yourself is just as bad as someone else laying one on you. Others may do it to control and manipulate you, threatening you with some form of punishment. When you do it to yourself, you are instigating the same form of threat; i.e., "If I don't do something, I must be a bad person." And when we expect some form of punishment, we will likely attract just that.

Jason was barely out of high school when he was driving home from school and had a car accident. His girlfriend, in the passenger seat at the time, was killed instantly. If only she hadn't been in the car. He couldn't move past it for a long time, even though there was nothing he could do about it then or now. Jason felt guilty until I explained to him that guilt was the flip side of blame. Either someone else is blaming you in order to make you feel guilty so they can control you, or you are blaming yourself, which gives others the opportunity to blame you, so you can control them.

Another reason a lot of people feel guilty is that they weren't there when the person they cared for passed away. I had a client whose son was terminally ill. The son was in a coma for weeks, and she was there by his side night after night. Unfortunately, the one night that she went home to get some much needed rest in her own bed, he passed away. It wasn't until I met her years later that she finally let go of the guilt by forgiving herself.

Another form of guilt is survivor's guilt. Losing loved ones through an accident, death, homicide, suicide, illness, or any other unexpected form of loss can cause one to feel guilty for not having it happen to them. Even something as simple as being the "normal" child in a family with a special needs child can cause one to feel less deserving and bring on such feelings like *I cannot and will not succeed. If something good happens to me, I should not feel worthy and celebrate.* If they celebrate or feel good about themselves, they believe they would have betrayed their loved one or other members of the family. Such people continually try to punish themselves for something they never had control over in the first place.

If one is suffering from survivor's guilt, they must intuitively touch base with their center and remember that we cannot be held responsible for anyone else's path. We must allow them the ownership of their own karma and stop using their experience as an excuse to stop living up to our own.

Unconditional Self-Acceptance

Just love yourself. There were times when that phrase just made me want to throw up. I was in the middle of hell, down on my knees wishing I could die, and I was supposed to love myself? Seriously? *Yes*, my divine guides assured me. Terrific. And how exactly was I supposed to accomplish something that sounded as foreign to me at the time as quantum physics? The best my guides could do was to tell me I was magnificent just the way I was. If I looked deeper, I would see the same.

I wasn't magnificent. I was an emotional wreck. I just couldn't see past the bend in the road. But eventually I reached inward, because I had nowhere else to go. When I did, I slowly navigated my way around the dark shadows and through the twists and turns that lay deep within the valley of my soul. The journey took time; I traversed through many narrow canyons with formidable walls, but eventually I came out into what I referred to as the clearing, an entirely new landscape I could call my life.

Condemning ourselves is almost self-indulgent. We can remain comfortable when we don't have to own up to our true selves and rely strictly upon our physical images. We can meditate, chant, and proclaim our spirituality, but as long as we have any self-judgments, awakening will be nothing but words. You must stop reproaching, criticizing, punishing, condemning, shaming, and belittling yourself. Why do we do that? Because if we did not, we would have to touch our own love, and if we touched that love we would destroy our images.

Our self-image lends us a form of false security. We know who we think we are, even if we know it's not the same as who we really are. There lies within each of us a power that creates a certainty, a knowing. Intuitively, when we discover this place within, we no longer need to hide behind our comfortable insecurities. Our only job is to find that place and stay there.

The truth is that…the truth hurts! But you know what? At least it's *your* truth and your truth alone. When we deny who we really are, we close ourselves off. You are not defined by your pain and disappointments. When you think you are, you ask for a new life while wondering if you even deserve it. You want a new life and might even see it right around the corner, yet you can't quite seem to figure out how to get from here to there. The only way out of this mess is to remember that you are a valuable, worthy being despite the pain—not because of it.

You must start to tell the truth about who you are not only to yourself, but to everyone else as well. Once you embrace who you are without expectations, pretenses, and the need to please anyone else, you will find true freedom.

You can't judge yourself and accept who you are simultaneously. Being self-accepting is a way of life. You have to be true to yourself despite your circumstances and what anyone is saying about you. What you think of yourself is your business and no one else's. Empowerment becomes ours when we can stand in the presence of our own love, without running away.

Self-denigrating is only keeping us from the realization that we are the very essence of the source of all things. Forget and let go of who you used to be, and become who you want to be. In this space, you realize that life is full of loss and change. In this space, not only can you deal with your sadness, but you can begin to experience a new type of joy. By renewing and transforming, you can find the spiritual magic of acceptance.

Once we transcend who we once believed ourselves to be or how we think we should be, we actualize our future. And that future is filled with peace, freedom, wholeness, and love.

If this is hard for you, remember that you did the best you could in all the situations that have arisen in your life so far. Even if you made mistakes, hopefully they were opportunities for you to grow and learn. Instead of getting bitter, you got better. Love the person you are despite your mistakes. Now, go into your inner self and give yourself a big hug.

EXERCISES

Meditation: How to Really Forgive

How do we do it? For starters we simply have to be willing to forgive. Sound a bit too simple? Maybe, but really it is that easy.

Melissa had just completed a seven-year divorce. She could not find a way to forgive her ex-husband for putting her "through the wringer," only to be left with next to nothing. The awful truth crashed into her somewhat ambiguous self-sufficiency.

I suggested a simple technique. I asked her to find a quiet place, close her eyes, and picture herself being surrounded by goodness and light. After she felt completely relaxed, I asked her to think of the man who made her so angry, who hurt her so deeply. I then asked that she also try to see his humanity.

When she felt she had, I asked her to get into a quiet, meditative state. Once she was completely relaxed, I asked that she continue breathing deeply and repeat the following:

I forgive _____ (who you choose to forgive) for _____ (whatever they did). Then, I forgive myself for judging _____ (same person) for doing _____ (same thing).

Most people want to skip the second sentence, but this is the most important part. In order to heal, it's imperative that you acknowledge that you are not only judging the other person for their actions, but judging yourself for your own. I asked her to do this every day for twenty-one days. Each time she did it, she felt as if a layer of hatred had been lifted from her. At the end of the twenty-one days, she felt lighter and free.

Forgiveness is like a muscle; the more you exercise it, the stronger it will get. Forgive anyone who hurt you, or against whom you are holding a grudge from any time in your life. If no other person was involved—for instance, if you feel you failed, made a mistake, or transgressed in any way—the process remains the same. First you must grant yourself forgiveness for whatever failing you had and then also forgive yourself for passing judgment.

In the spiritual sense, there isn't any real sin; there is only a temporary indiscretion. There are higher levels of action and lower levels. In this lifetime, I guarantee you will be responsible for inflicting and receiving both. In one particular instance, you chose the lower road, but you mustn't beat yourself up. You haven't really failed. All you've done is gone from one end of the spiritual spectrum to the other. We have to understand contrast in order to learn. If you put your trust in your inner guides, you will become stronger and not repeat the same mistake again. You will understand that you were being shown there is a different path you can walk, and had you not done what you did, you may never have learned of it. Symbolically draw a line in the sand, and then step across it to the other side. On this side of the road, it won't happen again.

We're not perfect. We are all human. Forgive yourself for being human, and for your humanness. Then you can move on.

Journaling: Make It Write

If you are still having a hard time forgiving, write the person or thing a letter. One woman I know wrote a letter of forgiveness to her breasts shortly after a double mastectomy. I loved the letter, because she thanked them for being a part of her life for so long, and was grateful that once they were removed, the cancer was gone. If it's a person you're having a difficult time with, write the letter as if you want to forgive them, even if you don't. You're not done yet, however. After the letter is written, you must write the reply that person or thing would send back to you.

Start your letter. Discuss the wounds that were inflicted on you, and the wounds you may have inflicted upon others as a result. When you finish it, I would like you to read it a few times, perhaps even aloud to a trusted friend. Then stash it away for a few days. After you've done that, I'd like you to write the reply. It doesn't matter if you wrote to a house you moved away from, or someone who died or left you. You must imagine being the other party and answering the letter that you sent.

If you feel vulnerable or weak, remind yourself that this will only make you stronger. Let the anger go and release it back to the universe to deal with. The other person is on their own path and they will get what they deserve in the end. If there is a deeper reason for the hurt, it should come out in the letter you write. You may not want to write the letter, but do it anyway, even if you don't feel forgiving. Write it as if you truly do want to forgive that person. In doing so, you will heal yourself more than the one you are forgiving. If the person you need to forgive is deceased, write the letter as if you could still send it to them.

Here's an example of a letter a client wrote to her ex-husband many years ago, along with the letter she imagined receiving in reply:

Dear John,

You bastard! I don't think I could ever forgive you for what you did to me. It's hard for me to remember that in the beginning of our marriage, I loved you so much, and I thought you loved me. I think it's knowing just how much I loved you that tore me to pieces. It might sound funny to you, or weird even, but you may as well have killed me. That's how I feel, as if there is a part of me that has been murdered. I cry all the time. After you left, I felt so sad and angry. Sometimes I still do, even though it's been almost two years.

I tried to put my life back together, but that's not as easy as it sounds. I don't have any friends. The friends we had together seemed to want nothing to do with me anymore. The few other friends I have are married, and they kind of look at me as if I am some kind of leper and they might catch my disease. I think they think I might rub off on them, and they don't want me around them or their husbands. It's strange how they acted. They just sort of wrote me off. I can't even go to the same doctor. He wanted to talk about you, even though I said that I wouldn't.

I don't miss you anymore. But I do miss having someone around, someone to talk to, even though we didn't talk that much. Right now, I couldn't even imagine going out with another man or dating. I don't believe that there are any good men out there anymore. Maybe, someday I won't feel that way, but right now I do.

I hope I find happiness. I think you already have, since you got married almost right away. That hurt me too, that you could just forget me so quickly, toss me away, and move on like that. For a long time, I was convinced you would treat her the same way you did me and that she would leave you. I secretly hoped she would. I don't feel that way anymore. I'm not sure I can say I want you to be happy, but I don't want you to suffer either.

It's time for me to get on with my own life and discover more of who I really am. I wish you well, and I really do mean that.

Sincerely,
Beverly

———

Dear Beverly,

I'm sorry that you are so hurt. I didn't mean for that to happen, but the truth is that we weren't getting along for a long time. You were moody all the time and you would fly off the handle over nothing. Absolutely nothing. So emotional. I just stopped talking. Okay, maybe I shouldn't have done that, but that's it; that's all I could do. You make it sound as if I had another choice, but I didn't. I had to leave. And if I didn't leave, I think you would have. I was getting older, and I felt like I couldn't live like that anymore. I had to leave. I hope someday you are happy like I am.

Sincerely,
John

By writing these two letters, Beverly was able to intuitively connect with the anger she had festering deep within her. Her fear really came from being alone. And by writing the second letter, she could even see where she had gone wrong in the marriage and was finally able to let it go. Beverly went back to nursing school, which she had never completed, and got a job at a hospital in her community. She has since decided to get a degree in psychology so she can help counsel other women who are going through what she went through. She hasn't dated extensively yet, but the last time I checked, she was willing to open herself up to the idea once again.

Although this may be jarring at first, if you do this exercise openly and honestly, you might just find a piece of the puzzle that was there all along and finally get a clearer picture of the past. I've done this myself. Suddenly I didn't feel betrayed or angry anymore. I felt, well, I felt…relieved. It was as if an elephant had been sitting on my chest for years and finally it decided to get up and walk away. I could breathe.

Here's the trick. As I said, I wrote about how I *felt.* I wasn't writing about what I thought. Often we get the two mixed up. We may say we feel a certain way, when in fact we are not feeling it, but thinking it. Saying that you feel you should get a new job, or feel you should take a vacation, isn't really how you feel. It's what you *think* you should do. Next time you catch yourself writing or saying something you believe describes how you feel, try substituting the words "I think" and see if this isn't more appropriate. Likewise, if you say you think you are depressed, it makes more sense to say you feel depressed. It's important, because feeling is healing.

Spiritual Practice: Heaven's Gate

If you really want to love yourself, you're going to have to search deep down in your soul. In short, you must turn around and face yourself. No matter how embarrassing it feels or how much you want to hide certain aspects of yourself, you must face your inner conscience. Only you can do this and you alone. Friends are able to do many things for us in the midst of despair; they can shield us from pain and sympathize with our situation. But no one can account for yourself the way you can. It's a moral decision that sets your own mind at peace. The thoughts are yours alone, and though they may be torturous, you must face them deliberately. By facing yourself head on, you will discover that you are perfect exactly as you are.

Find an entrance with which you feel connected. It could be the gate to a garden, a doorway into your spiritual sanctuary, or the entrance to a building that makes you feel strong and alive. Now stand in front of that entrance and imagine that your higher power is on the other side of that entrance. This higher power says to you, "Here you are at the gates of Heaven. All you have to do is confess what you hate about yourself, and I will let you in!"

What would you say? Take a minute to think about it. Now, if you can say it aloud, do so. If not, internally tell your higher power exactly what it is. Then walk through that entrance and be done with it. Walk through the gates of Heaven now. There is no need to wait.

Living in the
Divine Now

If you want to change who you are, start by changing your time zone. By living in the now, we literally disarm the ego. Intuitively, we let go of past mistakes that continually haunt us and stop fantasizing about a future that doesn't exist. Both of these fears keep us on the edge of reality, instead of the center of our being.

To dive into our real lives means that we stop looking outward in anticipation of what will happen later or looking inward to understand what the heck happened before. Our attention must stay in the here and now. It isn't as easy as we think. But if we allow our innate gifts to come forward, we have all the awareness necessary to go with the flow.

The universe is eternal. Therefore, the only point where eternity meets time is in the present moment. If that's true, then the only time that really exists is right now. If you think about it, what you did two seconds ago is already a part of your past. Being in the now and letting our natural abilities guide us will set our spirits free. When we relax into the now without stewing about the past and worrying about the future, opportunities naturally come our way. The shackles of self-imposed limitations fall away. That's because our capacity to shine brilliantly is equal to our capacity to disengage with time as we know it. The biblical statement "time shall be no more" means that we will one day live fully in the present, without obsessing about the past or future.

The only purpose of the past is that it got us where we are. The past is literally all in our heads, and if you think about it, most of it isn't even real anymore, just our perceptions of what we thought was real to us. If you are anything like me, you know how it is to feel trapped within your own skin and thoughts while going through any type of transition. There was the lingering confusion of what happened and the continuing anxiety of what hadn't happened yet. If we can intuitively cross the bridge between the cold, hard world of the past and the nerve-jangled anticipation of the future, we can bring both into the present moment. Ethereally, we redefine pieces of history, even the parts that haven't occurred yet.

The beauty of this is that in any given moment, we are given a clean slate. We can once again choose to write the story of our lives. The trouble is that most people don't buy into it. This is when I typically hear someone say, "Yes, but..." There's too much stuff they can't seem to let go of in order to start over. The way around this is to abolish regrets that start with all the things that we think we should have done and didn't do, and all the things we did do, but that we think we didn't do correctly. Everyone has something they regret, whether they admit it or not. It doesn't matter if it was yesterday or ten years ago. If you live in the present moment, you give yourself permission to begin again.

We can't alter the past, but we can make peace with it. We can't alter the future, but we can become peaceful with it. When you come to know that your eternal being—your center—remains the same in all places in time, you create an intuitive safety net. By knowing that your inner guide brought you where you are today, you come to understand that the same inner guide will take you exactly where you need to go. If you fall, you will hit the net in the center of your being. No harm can come to you.

We've all had moments in our lives when we wanted to be somewhere else instead of where we were, or someone else instead of who we are. I remember that when I was younger, I couldn't wait to grow up. Then when I got my first job and apartment, I couldn't wait to be married. When I got married, I couldn't wait to have children. I never stopped to take in and relish where I was and who I was at the time. It wasn't until I reached my forties that I decided that I didn't want to regret not living in wonder of my life exactly as it was. We all go through stages, but the truth is, every stage is magnificent just the way it is if we just relax and enjoy it, instead of hurrying to become who we think we are supposed to be.

As Jesus said in his sermon on the mount, "Be ye not anxious for tomorrow, for tomorrow shall be anxious for itself." There is no way for you to know what's going to happen tomorrow, or the next day, or five years from now. Only your ego speculates about the possibilities, because it's the only way it knows how to keep you slightly frantic and paranoid. You can't believe you'll be happy if it's always out there somewhere. If you have faith and trust, you'll know that the universe will take care of the future for you.

We may want a new beginning, but we try to create a future from the darkness of the past. We base our reality on the perception of what has happened in the past, carry that forward into the present, and thus create a future not unlike the past. If we felt we were lacking in our past and believe it in the present, nothing in our life will change. We're simply trying to compensate for what we don't have instead of creating what we want. The past, present, and future become a continuation of the other unless we stop it from happening. The only place we can break this vicious cycle is in the Divine Now.

What is the Divine Now? It's not exactly the present, insomuch as the second something happens, it's already part of the past. To me, the Divine Now is the unknown and living within it. It is the ultimate definition of faith. When we are able to simply trust that we are perfect beings in the perfect place at the perfect time for our own higher good, magic happens. There is so much potential lying dormant within you. All you have to do is listen to your inner voice. It will tell you that all is well.

When we are constantly centering in the past or future, we fall asleep and don't notice that everything we are seeking is right in front of us. In the beauty of the moment, we can accept ourselves exactly as we are and have more energy to give to life. We are not wasting our time trying to change our circumstances. The moment we relax into the deeper ground of our being, giving up the struggle to be anywhere else, we are intuitively sent to the right place at the right time.

If you have a hard time believing this, go outside and look at all that surrounds you. There is a great gift there waiting for you to open your arms and embrace it. The very essence of nature lies within the Divine Now. Examine a tiny flower with its exquisite symmetry and color. It doesn't question itself. It just is. Allow your heart to expand and reach out to all that is about you, the grass, the trees, the shrubs, the birds, the bees, and everything that you cannot see. Feel their state of purity and knowing. Feel the love that engulfs you. Feel that peace.

As you have created this precious moment, realize that you create all the moments to come by being who you are now. Stay perfectly conscious of everything happening to you in this moment, inside and out…and the next moment, and the next. Pay attention to NOW, and tomorrow you will drift happily through the rest of today.

Creating a New Normal

What exactly is normal? Normal is what your life used to be like before you went through whatever you went through. Now how do you create a new life when the previous life was blown to smithereens? Really, this is what this whole book is about—creating a new you, reinventing yourself.

One client, Bob, had spent all of his holidays with his wife and kids, but when his wife passed away and his children left home, he decided that his new normal would be traveling to a city he had never been to before and enjoying the Christmas lights. The first place he went was Paris. After that, it was New York, and who knows where he will go next year. He's not sure, but he knows he will book a trip somewhere even if it's close to home, because this has now become his new tradition.

The most difficult part of creating a new normal is emotionally letting go of the old normal. Trying to hold on to whatever made your life normal before your loss is a way of not acknowledging the reality of what happened to you.

We've already talked about letting go, but we must also begin planting the seeds of wanting a new normal. Keeping your husband's ashes in an urn next to your bed is probably not a good idea. Leaving your wife's clothes in her closet after she has passed on isn't either. Driving by the house you used to live in before the foreclosure is not a good plan. Facebook stalking your ex-lover has to stop.

Start to see yourself in your new life. Visualize it. See what parts of it are gone and what has been added. You can create another life, and it will be … normal.

EXERCISES

Meditation: Meeting Your Past and Future Selves
When you have quieted your mind and feel completely relaxed, allow your intuitive mind to carry you back in time to when you were young. Ask yourself the following questions:

- How do you look? What do your facial features look like, your hair, your clothes?

- How do you feel? What are you thinking about right now at the age that you chose to be?

- Why did you pick this time and place to revisit yourself?

- What did you enjoy doing when you were this age?

- What did you hate about being this age?

- What excited you the most?

- What scared you the most?

- What skills did you acquire that helped you become who you are?

Have a conversation with your younger self. Let your memories and emotions flow freely. Do not try to suppress any thoughts or feelings. Be completely honest with yourself. Thank the person you once were, because she taught you a lot. Forgive her and know that she did the best she could at the time. Above all, when your conversation is over, remember to tell her just how much you love her.

Now, allow images of yourself growing older to come to your mind. Imagine how you will be ten, fifteen, or twenty years from now. Ask yourself the following questions:

- How do you look? Again, describe your facial features, your hair, your clothing. What does your body look and feel like?

- How do you feel?

- What have you accomplished in your life?

- What do you wish you had accomplished in your life?

- What do you dream about?

- Who have you loved and who do you love now?

- Is there something you fear?

- What are you grateful for?

- Do you have any regrets?

Have a warm and loving conversation with the person that you have become. Ask her what advice she would give you to get you through the transition you have been through or are now in. Is there anything that she feels you should be handling differently in your life right now?

When you feel you have completed the conversation, again be certain to end it in a kind and loving way. You love who you have become, and she loves you exactly the way you are right now.

Stepping back and looking at yourself objectively will make you aware of the astounding changes that have taken place, and that will take place over time. Besides looking within, also take some time in the meditation to really explore the relationships you have had with the important people in your life. Picture your family, friends, and anyone else who has affected you so far and who might in the future. Are you reacting to them differently now than you will later?

Over the next few days, expect more images and thoughts to surface. With this meditation, fresh insights will appear every day. Do not dismiss the ideas that will color your mind. Together they are the materials you will use to create pieces of a puzzle. Each thought contains another clue to the bigger picture that is your life. When you put the jigsaw pieces together, you will have a clearer picture of who you *are*—not then and not in the future—but now. And that's all that counts.

Journaling: No Regrets

I remember when my mother used to say, "Put that candy down! You have no idea where it came from," and then she'd slap my hand. Of course, she was right.

Well, you can feel that way about a lot of the regrets you've picked up along the way in your life. Who knows where they came from? Sometimes, we don't even know what they are anymore. Maybe they were important at the time, so we stashed them away in the pockets of our subconscious. Years later, they're still there, except now they are sticky, half-melted balls of gunk.

A regret is simply a string of thoughts you keep pulling together. Without knowing it, you then find yourself thinking a particular way and wondering why you're not feeling so hot. It can usually be attributed to an antiquated belief, hidden away in the attic in your head.

Once you understand this, you can intuitively pinpoint your outdated habits of thinking. Next time your emotions begin to crawl with sorrow and remorse for all the things you wished you had done or didn't do, ask your inner guidance if it's an old pattern of thought coming back to haunt you. Your inner self is naturally fighting what it knows to be in direct contradiction to your truth. When you know the supposed cause of however you're feeling is no longer a truth, you can override it by pulling yourself back into the present moment, where all healing occurs.

Think about something you regret and write it down. Now write the following statement, "Maybe I should have (insert what you wished you would have done), but I don't care anymore. From now on I will create (insert what you believe you can do differently)."

After many failed relationships, Allison truly felt she would never have a healthy, loving, committed relationship. Here's what she said: "Maybe I should have married John, but I didn't, and I don't care anymore. From now on I will create the relationship I want and deserve."

Ed never felt he could do what he loves for a living and still make a lot of money. Here's what he said: "Maybe I should have tried being an artist. I don't care anymore, and from now on I will try to sell as much of my artwork as possible."

This exercise brings you back to the Divine Now, where you are directly connected to your core energy, which is the ultimate point of power.

Spiritual Practice: Pleasantly Present

We vow that "next week" (the ugly stepchild of "later") we will begin to pay attention to the things and people that really matter. But next week or later never arrives. Let's face it, most of us rarely if ever appreciate what we have until it is gone. Country music wouldn't exist if this weren't true.

We must intuitively learn to shift our perspective to knowing that this moment is all that matters—right here, right now—to awaken to life's magnificence. This means that we have to stop being preoccupied with our daily to-do lists. It also means that we have to stop becoming engrossed in rewriting the past and daydreaming about the future. Only by stopping the internal commentary we've become immersed in which has nothing to do with what's going on in the moment will we no longer live in a make-believe world of our own imagining. If we don't, we are robbing ourselves of living in this present moment, of receiving its gifts as they pass by unnoticed.

Simply become aware of your surroundings: the sights, the sounds, even the silence. Take a "Be Present" break several times a day, and just become aware of what is happening right here, right now. You will be in the Divine Now. You will be in the moment. Try to keep yourself there.

Part Three

Transitioning

It may not be wise to
live beyond your means,
but it's always wise to
live beyond your meaning.

Seven

Spiritual Solutions

I once told a client that she really needed to be more positive about her relationships with men. Her answer was, "Yes, I am. I am absolutely positive that I will never fall in love again."

"Just change your thinking," people say. "Move on," others say. "Write new affirmations," say the spiritual among us. But honestly, we are never really going to completely wipe out the memory of the pain of our losses, and we probably shouldn't. But how do we transform our own personal sorrows into meaningful growth and transformation? How do we find peace, harmony, and acceptance within the framework of our day-to-day world?

The poet John Keats wrote a letter in 1819. In it he referred to the world not as a vale of tears, but as "the vale of soul-making." He went on to say, "Do you not see how necessary a world of pains and troubles is to school an intelligence and make it a Soul? A place where the heart must feel and suffer in a thousand diverse ways!"

We know intuitively that the events of our lives are not arbitrary. However intangibly, we feel connected to a higher self, unraveling the mysteries in our own lives. As we become more spiritually evolved, we become more determined to find wisdom and reach a deeper understanding of our lives and our paths.

Pain and loss impel us to look inward. Where else can we go? If we use our intuition to look inside our own lives, I truly believe we will come up with the answers we need. I have, so I know you can. Nobody else can become another person's answer person. Every spiritual master I have ever encountered all taught me one thing, that the answers you discover for yourself will always be worth more than anybody else's.

Some people say the purpose of life is to serve a higher power, some say it is to love and be loved, and others say it is simply to procreate. But really, I believe that it is to know oneself, because without that internal self-actualization, nothing else works. When we know ourselves, we can recognize our own inner wisdom and our own divine light. And when we recognize it in ourselves, we can see that light shining within everyone else. Acceptance, compassion, and forgiveness are a natural outcome of discovering our true selves. Pleasure and pain will come and go, but the self-realization you gain in the process will stay with you for all eternity.

Go Ahead and Lose Your Mind

Part of our human survival mechanism is to mentally process everything. Thinking sets up an entire set of neurons that fire and wire together to help us function and learn. The trouble is when we think in a logical, practical way, we slam the door on our higher knowing. We are so unsure of ourselves in the arena of trusting our inner guidance that when an inspired thought comes in, more times than not we'll try to intellectualize or override it to feel secure and safe.

We have a mind, but we are not a mind. We are spirit. Our mind is meant to be a servant to the spirit, not vice versa. When we defend ourselves by being rational, thinking through things over and over again, we block out our inner voice completely and the truth is lost. We move in a direction we "think" would be good for us, instead of what we "know" would be a mistake. The logical mind causes us to second-guess what we feel, and suddenly we don't trust ourselves anymore. We start to say things like, "I can't do this. I don't think I'm good enough. I don't want to surrender."

Right about then is when you should just go ahead and lose your mind. When you push against yourself, you will struggle. When you surrender to life, you will move effortlessly with the flow. As you start to live from your intuition, you give up thinking in the traditional sense. You focus on the energy of each moment, allowing things to unfold as you go. In this way, you are led in the direction that is right for you, as things are handled in their own time and way.

Now you can and will experience resistance. Your friends and family might question why you would want to sell your home so you can travel the world. A colleague may call you nuts when you mention that you don't really want that promotion and actually, you're not even sure that you want the job anymore. Everyone else may think that you need your head examined, especially if you tell them that you will trust your gut and you know that something good will come out of that.

Remember this: THIS IS YOUR LIFE TO LIVE AS YOU WANT TO LIVE IT. Not how your mother wants you to live it, your best friend, or the person who sits in the cubicle next to yours. As you learn to access and act upon the wisdom of the universe, you will find that your fear slips away and you can move forward with confidence in the directions of your dreams.

Tame Your Monkey Mind

You create your thoughts. Your thoughts create your will. Your will creates your intentions. Your intentions create your action. Your actions create your destiny.

Meet Jane. Jane was literally sick with worry. She was laid off from her job a month after purchasing a new home.

She found herself in a state of constant anxiety over what she hoped wouldn't happen. She was so filled with fear about not finding a new job and possibly losing her beautiful new home that she couldn't think about anything else. She came to me to find out how she could stop this constant cycle of panic and fear. I told her to stop worrying. She laughed and said, "That's easy for you to say, isn't it?"

Well, yes, it is easy for me to say! And it could be for her as well, if she would listen. Where you put your thoughts will be what you create. The more you point out what you don't want, the more of it you'll get. I asked her to try an experiment. Every time she had a negative, worried thought, she should simply catch herself and replace it with a positive one, either of what she did want or of gratitude for what she still had. I also gave her a mantra to repeat if she couldn't think of anything: "Everything I want and need is now coming to me." Twenty-four hours was all I asked for. When she called and said she actually tried it, I encouraged her to do it again, but this time for a week. At the end of the week, she felt much calmer and had even scheduled two interviews. New opportunities were coming her way.

Your thoughts are seeds that you plant every minute of every day. And what you plant in your mind grows and attracts your experiences. If you plant apple seeds, you are going to get an apple tree, not a lemon or oak tree. Whether you plant seeds of worry and fear, or seeds of hope and joy, your life will bear the fruit of those thoughts. If you let your thoughts run rampant, they'll bang around all over the place, much like a wild monkey in a china shop.

Ernest Holmes said, "Where your mind goes, energy flows." When you pay attention to your thoughts, what do you hear yourself saying about your life? Eavesdrop on your thoughts and listen carefully. These are the beliefs you hold.

Your mind is only capable of having one thought at a time. Make it count. Whatever you concentrate on, you empower. So if you've been concentrating on negative or adverse things, they will become a reality. If you say "this job is a pain in the ass," don't be surprised if you suddenly get hemorrhoids. If you affirm lack, opportunities pass you by, money falls out of your wallet, someone steals your car. You get the idea.

Discipline your mind, and cut out any deprecating statements, especially ones that destroy your energy and make you sick. If someone asks you how you feel, say, "Fantastic!" So I want you to lie, you ask? In this case, yes, lie your heart out. You change how you feel by how you think, and you change how you think by how you feel. We are neurologically wired that way. At first your mind may resist. It might say something like, "I don't feel fantastic, I feel like crap." Resist it. It may be a bit of a battle at first, but that's the challenge of this sacred journey. Do not let yourself be victimized by your mind. You can push back and change its programming. Don't fight it, but gently disempower its negative influence. Use your inner guidance system to put the "monkey mind" back in its place, behind a locked door. You'll find that it is much easier to create the life you want by tapping into your inner wisdom when the monkey is no longer jumping up and down and screaming in your ear.

I used to have a teacher who intuitively knew when I was tumbling thoughts around in my head. She would stop me and tell me to quiet my mind and pick up one thought at a time. Once I did, I realized the thoughts that were popping into my head were involuntary. All I was doing was scratching at them like a bad bug bite, irritating them further. She suggested I stretch my arms out and squeeze the air as if I were grabbing hold of one of those thoughts in my head. Once I had a tight grip, she'd have me open my hands and release it to the universe. "It's out of your hands now, isn't it?" she would say. And she was right.

Live Dangerously

It is said that Nietzsche used to have a sign on his wall that said LIVE DANGEROUSLY. Someone once asked him why and he reportedly said, "Just to remind me, because my fear is tremendous."

We all have fears. And we all do things we don't want to, but continue to out of fear. But if we stay in these comfort zones, especially when they are no longer comfortable, we start to die inside. A girlfriend of mine wanted to take her five-year old daughter, Emma, to Disneyland and asked if I cared to join them. I love Disneyland, so of course I leapt at the opportunity to unleash my inner child. We took her

daughter on all the rides, and she was ecstatic. At the end
of the day, Emma turned to her mother and said, "Gee,
Mom, did you use to have such a good time in the olden
days when you used to be alive?"

My girlfriend was stunned. But the truth of the matter
is that she had died inside a long time ago. She had settled into a life of security, comfort, and convenience, even
though that's not really what she wanted for herself or her
family. Somewhere in that rut, she'd stopped living.

Later, she asked me if I could show her the way out,
but I told her that the way was not out, but in . . . within. If
she truly listened to what her inner guidance system was
telling her, she would discover all the answers she needed.
No one can really tell you your answer but yourself. All I
can do is teach you how to reach in there, into your true
authentic self. It is our own fear that stops us from living
dangerously, as Nietzsche said. And the truth is, he knew it
wasn't dangerous. It was just different.

A line in a Rumi poem reads, "Move within, but don't
move the way fear makes you move." More than seven
hundred years have passed since Jalal al-Din Muhammad
Rumi wrote these words, and they are still true. What I
believe Rumi meant here is that we should only move the
way love makes us move, the way joy makes us move.

After we left Disneyland, I asked my girlfriend to
do one thing for me, and that was to find time every day
to meditate on being fearless, taking a few minutes every
day to not ask for anything or feel guilty for not doing

something she thought she should have been doing, and just be. All she had to do was go inward and listen to that small, still voice. As she did this, she became much more joyful and as she put it, "a space opened up inside of me that felt wider than the sky." Follow your inner voice, listen to what's in your heart, and then move toward it.

Living dangerously has nothing to do with going out and doing something crazy. It has to do with going within and asking yourself what you would do if you knew you couldn't fail; what you would be if you knew you could be anything. It's about becoming who you really are.

A Leap of Faith

There's an old Zen story about a man who was walking along a path at night. Suddenly, he slipped and fell off the edge. Somehow he managed to grab hold of a branch. In the darkness of the night, all he could see below him was a bottomless abyss. Scared to death, he held on for dear life. His hands started to grow cold, and his grip loosened. Fearing he would die, he shouted out to the universe, "If there is anyone up there that can tell me what to do."

He heard a voice that he could only imagine to be God. "Just let go."

Let go? Let go?! He couldn't imagine letting go and falling to his death. "Let go?"

"Yes," the voice repeated. "Just let go."

He thought about this carefully, his fingers straining to hold on. "Is there anyone else up there I can talk to?"

Dead silence.

So the man hung there all night long, living a nightmare. When the sun finally appeared he looked down to see what was below him. It turned out that the ground was only a few inches from his feet.

———————

It's up to you whether or not you want to cling to the branch and live in a nightmare, and whether you have enough trust and faith to simply let go.

When you move through your challenges, remember that your inner guidance system will never let you down. As you take action on your dreams, you may feel as if you are on the edge of a cliff and you are about to take a leap of faith, and no one is there to catch you. But it could be that your fear is only a few inches deep. The inspiration and direction from your intuition is there to guide you safely to your hopes and dreams.

The tough thing about intuition is that we know, but we don't know *how* we know. And sometimes we don't even know what we know. But what if my ideas aren't really inspired? What if they're coming from my need to fix something? How can I trust that what I'm getting is coming from my expanded self or those around me?

When we get an intuitive hit, that's the time we often start to question it. But that's really the time not to. Believing that we'll be judged somehow, we become paralyzed by the idea that we might make a mistake. This is the ego speaking. There is no such thing as a mistake, only lessons we must learn. Yet we want verification that what we're getting is the real deal instead of more of our fears. What we want is a guarantee.

The universe is not going to give you a certificate. What it will give you is a feeling. All you have to remember is that if it feels good, it's the right thing to do. If it doesn't feel good, it's not the right thing to do.

Nothing is more valuable than trusting our impulses, it's our direct connection to infinite intelligence that can give us all the answers to any problem we ever had, or ever will have. Put forth the intent that you are going to learn to trust the ideas that give you a twinge of excitement. They fly in on the wings of positive energy.

So, if your grandmother is speaking to you in your dreams, pay attention to the message. Listen to what the dear departed one is saying. If you suddenly know something before it happens, act upon it. If you get information from out of the blue, trust that it is a sign that you must do something about it.

Joan Borysenko said, "One doesn't have to be holy and healed to experience divine guidance. In fact, such guidance often comes as a result of pain and problems…when things are coasting along smoothly we don't need guidance. The sudden flashes of intuition and dreams we have in our darkest hours, however, are capable of renewing our lives, changing our course, and mending a broken spirit."

Checking In

The value of reflection and self-examination is certainly one of the roots of healing. When we learn to check in consistently with our inner wisdom, we own what has happened to us, making it much easier for us to process and move through it.

Practice checking in with your inner guidance system on a regular basis. It doesn't matter if you do it once a day or once an hour, as long as you do it. All you have to do is stop and take a few minutes to relax and listen to your gut feelings. You don't always have to be sitting by candlelight in a cross-legged position with incense wafting through the air to touch base with your inner guidance system. I have a client who connects with her higher self when she stops at a red light. Well, not every time, but more times than not. She'll take a second to have a little chat with her inner self, just to make sure she's on track and doesn't get stressed out. She'll often remind herself that she'll get where she's going when she gets there and not any sooner by getting frustrated or upset.

If I am really stressed out, I check in more often. It almost sounds counterintuitive, but it is during my busiest times that I make the most time to stop and have a conversation with my higher self. Otherwise, I'm a wreck by noon and a total basket case by the end of the day. I probably shouldn't admit this, but while I am out in public, I will often take an extra minute or two in the ladies' room to not only freshen my makeup, but freshen my spirit as well. I take a deep, cleansing breath and center myself. It works wonders, trust me.

Cultivate the habit of having an intimate conversation with your inner self. Ask for help and guidance when you need it, and practice listening for answers, which may come in the form of words, images, feeling, or being led to an external source such as a book, friend, or teacher. Listen to your body, and see if it is trying to give you a message. If you are uncomfortable or in pain, it may be because you are ignoring some important information the universe is trying to give you.

Living in the Light

Anne Frank said, "Everyone has inside of him a piece of good news. The good news is that you don't know how great you can be! How much you can love! What you can accomplish! And what your potential is!"

No matter what life has handed you so far, you have the opportunity to find pleasure, love, joy, and a renewed sense of purpose. Dance and laugh. Take some risks. Try new things. Understand that the disappointments and challenges were there to help guide you to a fuller, richer life. When you listen to the small, still voice inside your soul, a new dream will emerge. You have access to the gift of divine intuition to guide you to the fulfillment of that dream. Each time you ask for guidance and act on the wisdom you receive you align your mind with the mind of the universe. You tap into a stream of consciousness that will always provide exactly what you want and need.

You've done the best you could so far. You made choices and moved through your losses to the best of your abilities. The only challenge you have from now on is to live your life to the best of your abilities.

EXERCISES

Meditation: Cleaning Your Energy from the Inside Out
There is an electromagnetic field of energy flowing closely around your body, extending up to twelve inches in all directions. The ancient Greeks called it the etheric body, or subtle body, as they believed that the field is composed of a person's consciousness, their level of awareness. It's also more commonly called the aura.

Flashing through it are mini–lightning bolts of energy that flow out of your chakras. You actually walk around with an amazing bubble of light. When I do intuitive readings, the majority of the information I receive comes from the person's aura. You can't hide anything from your aura, as it will spill out of you whether you want it to or not. It overshadows our personality traits and weaknesses that arise from our human frailties. Though you wear your aura, it leaves you spiritually naked, as the very essence of our human experience is expressed within it.

The higher the state of your consciousness, the lighter and more clear your aura will be. The flow of energy will also be faster. That's why you attract positive energy when you feel happy, optimistic, or even hopeful.

When your consciousness is fearful, angry, sick, sorrowful, resentful, or vindictive, the aura becomes dark and slimy. It will hold negative thoughts in its field, making a person feel physically and emotionally depressed. A negative aura also attracts other people's negativity, which can congest it further. If we don't learn a lesson and we are carrying it around with us, it will sit in our aura and look quite similar to a big black hole. These holes are highly charged with whatever energy is necessary to draw to us the circumstances required for us to gain the emotional wisdom of the lesson. And they'll stay there, drawing new people, places, or things into our lives until we've owned the lesson.

But if you do gain the insight necessary to learn the lesson, the black hole will instantly dissipate, which means that you won't attract those conditions to you in the future. That's because when the black hole closes it allows more light, which is energy, into our beings, making it possible for us to feel and attract more positively.

Subliminally, we are aware of the energy around us, and the energy of those we encounter. Haven't you moved away from someone just because you didn't like their vibes? Something in their aura repelled you. If you have a sudden change of mood, for no apparent reason, often it is because someone is sending you negative energy, psychically attacking you.

My client Nora couldn't understand why she wasn't feeling well. Upon further investigation, I discovered Nora had just hired a new employee who really resented her. Nora knew this, but she didn't think it would affect her to this degree. After only two weeks, the rips and tears in Nora's aura grew larger and larger. Nora suggested that the woman be transferred to another department, which she was happy to do. Within days, Nora felt better. She said it felt as if someone had washed the windows to her soul and let the sunshine back in.

Becoming aware of your aura is easy. Close your eyes and breathe deeply. Now rub your palms together until they are warm, then shake your hands out. Rub them together again for a few seconds, and place them together in the prayer position. Now ever so slowly pull your palms apart, while they are still facing each other, until they are about six inches apart. Close your eyes and notice the pull of energy between your palms. This space between your palms is part of your aura.

To see your aura, relax your eyes and look into a mirror. Don't force it, but keep relaxing your eyes. Now look slightly to the right and look back at yourself without moving your eyeballs. Give it practice and time and you'll soon be able to see your aura. What color is it? Are there any shapes or dark spots? Any weak places? How far does it extend from your body?

It's important to keep on your toes and notice the tone and feel of your aura. It's like your own personal weather pattern, and like the weather, it changes. Fighting with someone will leave holes or weak spots, causing your equilibrium to shift off balance, leaving you vulnerable to sickness or depression. Holes and tears in the aura allow random consciousness floating around in the universe to seep into your personal space, which can wreak havoc on your mind and emotions.

Drug and alcohol abuse can rip the aura, requiring healing. Learning to receive love and release grudges will put your aura on the mend. Learning to love yourself is always an excellent antidote.

To cleanse your aura, close your eyes and relax your body, all the way from the tips of your toes up your feet, legs, stomach, arms, chest, neck, and head. Breathe deeply and each time you exhale, say, "I am letting go of any negativity."

When you feel you have quieted your body and mind, picture yourself in a beautiful field full of trees, flowers, and a beautiful stream. The sun is shining, the birds are singing, and you're walking toward the stream. You step into it, feeling the water on your feet. You walk along the stream until you come upon a waterfall. The water flowing down is colorful and bright, representing each of the colors of the chakras. You can see red and yellow and blue and green and orange and indigo and purple flowing down with the water.

As you breathe in, step under the waterfall and allow the water to flow over you and inside of you. Let the colors flow through your body. Let the blue calm your spirit, the green heal you, the indigo and purple increase your spirituality and intuition, and the red accelerate your healing and blood flow. As you exhale, let any particles that no longer belong in your body be released. Push them out into the water. Stay under the waterfall as long as you wish and then bring yourself back through the stream, across the fields of green, all the way back to yourself.

If you are around people you cannot avoid such as the controlling boss or the depressed spouse, don't forget to protect your aura. Imagine an energy field of white light surrounding your aura. Know that this shield will shut out the unwanted energy emitted from people, places, or things. Energy tends to hang in the air, and even places can have undesirable vibrations you may want to block.

Journaling: Automatic Answers

Whenever I have struggled with a question I couldn't find an answer to, I often use this technique to direct me to the "write" answer. This has also been referred to as automatic writing or directed writing, and is an ancient form of divination where messages are received from your higher source through your hand and onto paper.

Begin by finding a quiet spot, preferably at a desk or table where you'll be comfortable. Take a few minutes to relax your body and mind. With your eyes still closed, focus upon your hands. Internally "feel" your hands. Once you place your attention upon them you will sense the energy that radiates through them. Now direct the energy to your heart and "feel" your heart. A tingling sensation usually occurs in these areas of your body when you connect with the energy within. If it doesn't, please don't worry and continue. Now, connect your heart with your hands. Feel the energy flow between the two. Allow your fingers to wiggle if you have the need. Just relax and breathe deeply as you let your hands and your heart become one.

After a few minutes, take a deep cleansing breath and bring yourself back to reality. Gently place the pen to paper. Write a few sentences about what is concerning you in the moment. Explain the challenge you are facing in your life, as clearly and succinctly as you can. Now, form a question from what you have written. For example, if the challenge you are facing involves a divorce or separation and you are worried that you may never meet anyone ever again, then the question you would ask would simply be "Will I be in a loving relationship soon?"

Take another deep, relaxing breath. Now try not to focus on the paper and pen, just stare into the distance or at a specific object. If you find this difficult, you can always close your eyes again. Imagine that you are being surrounded by love and light. Call back the feeling of the energy moving between your hand and your heart, and begin writing. I personally love the principle of just letting it all come out until you are exhausted and then seeing what you've got at the end.

If nothing comes, do not be concerned. Forcing yourself to write something down would be counterintuitive. Be willing to wait in silence and allow the messages to come to you. Having the intention alone is enough to bring it about. Remember that intuition comes in many ways; you may not necessarily receive words to put on paper. You may be inspired to draw a picture, even if it's stick figures, a symbol of some sort, or a number that seems to resonate with you. Write down any impressions you get, no matter how far removed they seem from your question, or your life in general. There is no right or wrong way to do this, except to simply go with the flow, so don't stop. Trust in the universe and write what you might.

When you feel you are done, review what your hand has produced. Even if it seems like nonsense, try to decipher it as best as possible. Ask yourself if you are being guided by this intuitive insight, and if you are, what you should do next.

At this stage a lot of people tell me that they feel silly, as if they just made it all up. Yet when they analyze the impressions they recorded, they are shocked to find the answer to what they asked. And, when they acted on this information, their lives moved forward in a new and positive direction.

Spiritual Practice: Walking the Labyrinth

Labyrinths appear in many cultures and religious traditions. Native Americans used labyrinths to represent spiritual quests. There are many diverse patterns, from the earliest Greek labyrinths of 2500 BCE, to the medieval labyrinths laid in the floors of cathedrals in France and Italy.

A labyrinth is a complex, winding path that you walk, or trace with your finger. You can usually find one at a local spiritual center. In my own community there are several evening labyrinth walks where groups of people meet to walk the labyrinth together. I have watched groups create their own at a local park using rocks and stones. I also own several scarves with labyrinth prints on them which I trace with my finger during a meditation. Spiritual stores often carry printed paper ones as well. If there isn't a local labyrinth near you, consider creating your own. Just remember that the labyrinth is not a maze. It has no branches or dead ends. It is a path that usually leads you to a wider, open area in the center where one can meditate and rest.

Labyrinths are a metaphor for our spiritual journeys— reaching the center is the goal of both quests. We follow an unknown path that seems random, coming close to the center, only to find that we are back on the edge. The journey inward to the center is often described as a time to release and let go. The center is a place to listen and receive. The return journey can be a time of reflection, as steps are retraced that connect the quiet center with the outside world.

The labyrinth can be a way to further explore the gift of change in your life. As you walk the path of the labyrinth, meditate on a problem or repeat an affirmation or prayer. Think of your transition as a journey through a labyrinth. A labyrinth offers a type of walking meditation, and your emotions are much like the path. The twists and turns can be disorienting at first, until they become somewhat expected, and familiar. But you will not get lost as long as you stay on the path. There is nothing wrong with this process. It is as natural as the labyrinth itself.

Pause at the entrance before walking or tracing a labyrinth pattern with our finger. Release your concerns to the universe. Let go of any present expectations. Take slow, deep breaths. Quiet your mind. When you are ready, open your heart and enter the labyrinth. Walk comfortably and take with you a difficult loss in your life. As you experience the multiple turnings of the complex path, hold both the gift and your pain as loosely as you can.

When you reach the center of the labyrinth, take a deep breath and relax. Go inside to that still, quiet place of knowing. Now imagine yourself sitting in the center of a giant hourglass. Instead of sand, the hourglass is filled with white light. The top extends toward the heavens beyond your reach, and its bottom reaches down into the core of Mother Earth. Intensify the luminosity and fill it with a frequency of deep, deep love while you continue to feel yourself at the apex.

Now infuse the light with the frequency of appreciation through you from the heavens into the earth. Hold that vibration for as long as you can. Next, allow the frequency of gratitude to fill the funnel. Hold it for as long as you can.

Consciously let go of any worries and concerns, and bring yourself into the present moment. Pay attention to where you are right now. What will change as you move into the coming season? What will be lost? What will be gained? Are there things that you hold too tightly?

Now put yourself into the frequency of reverence, as if you are looking at the earth from outer space. Hold that feeling within your heart.

See and feel your divine hourglass of effervescent light fill with profound love: for humankind, love for the planet, love those who walk next to you, and, most importantly, for yourself. Let it wash throughout every inch of your body, every cell of your being, every atom of the air about you. Take your time and allow yourself to feel.

Lastly, feel the joy that fills your body and being. Hold on to that feeling for as long as you can. When you are ready, come on back.

Whether you know it or not, you have infused high frequencies of joy into yourself. And the higher your frequency, the greater your light will be. The greater your light, the stronger your power.

Pause, take a slow, deep breath. Settle into the silence. Give thanks to the universe for showing you how to let go of what no longer serves you before retracing your steps out into the world.

Eight

Saying Goodbye to Who You Used to Be

If you think about it, none of us are who we used to be. I was born, and then I was a toddler, child, teenager, and then an adult. When exactly did all of those things happen? At what point did I stop being a child? One day I'll be old. But when does that happen? Basically, it happens when we decide to let it happen.

Sometimes in the middle of the night, I think about the person I used to be. I think about my previous lives within this lifetime. I think about running away from home at the tender age of sixteen because I didn't want to be forced into an arranged marriage. I think about my first job at a newspaper where I learned to write and about life itself. All of this seems like a magical dream to me today, real as it was at the time. I am reminded of Buddha's words: "See this floating world as like a dream, like a mirage, like a fantasy." I wonder how much of what happened to me was real in the end.

On some level, we invented who we are—but don't get depressed yet! If this is true, we can reinvent ourselves any time we want. It's not as difficult as we make it out to be. We are all connected to people, places, things, and events. To some degree we even tend to define ourselves by these connections. But the truth is that all of these things—people, places, objects, ideas, accomplishments, habits, addictions, memories, and even opinions—represent our identity. We can intuitively change who we think we are by giving ourselves a going away party. When we do this, we will find that miracles of personal transformation do occur, and that we can have in life whatever we are willing to *be*.

We cling, crave, and lust for the things we desire; we avoid, get angry at, and hate those things we dislike. What do we want the most? What do we want the least? The only way we can free ourselves of these connections is to use our intuition to pay attention to the truth of what we wish to attract and what we wish to repel. If we do so correctly, we will not get lost in desiring things that are fleeting, clinging to things that are unreliable, both of which eventually set us up for a disappointment of some kind.

Identity is not so much about wanting and not wanting as it is about your feelings of what you want and don't want. If you are extremely attached to the house you live in and suddenly have to move, it will be a painful process. The pain won't be due to the change itself (which may eventually turn out to be good), but due to the fact that the house has become a part of your personality. If you remember that you are still the same person no matter what house you live in, it's not going to bother you. Nothing outside of you changes who you are.

You Already are Somebody

When John Donne said, "Ask not for whom the bell tolls, it tolls for thee," he was right on the money. During his lifetime, when people died there was a tradition: The bells in the churches would start tolling, informing the villagers that someone had died. It was a call to the people to return from their farms and work to give the person who had passed on a final send off.

Donne was right. We needn't send anyone to find out for whom the bell tolls. It is only ringing for us. Whenever someone passes from this earth, we are reminded that we are mortal beings, and death can take us anytime, anywhere it wants.

They say that the only real fear in life is the fear of death. If you become aware of this intuitively, it can't crush you. You can't be fearful if you know that there is nothing to fear. Some people try to make themselves into someone special and in a sense live forever. But, really, will life treat them any differently than it treats ordinary people? Life makes no discrimination, nor does death. It doesn't care if you are rich or poor, young or old, educated or uneducated. Death is the ultimate equalizer.

In India, there is a myth about a man who becomes a world conqueror. He surpasses even the title of king, or emperor. He is called a *chakravartin*. The name is derived from the Sanskrit words of *chakra*, meaning "wheel," and *vartin*, meaning "one who turns." Thus, a chakravartin is a ruler whose wheels of his chariot can roll around the earth without being obstructed. He is all-powerful.

The myth goes on to say that when a chakravartin goes to Heaven, he is treated like no other. He is granted access to a golden mountain that no one else is privileged to, for the eyes of a mere mortal could not take in the vastness and grandness of such a sight. The gold mountain is called Sumeru, and the chakravartin alone is allowed to sign his name upon it to prove how powerful he was for all eternity.

While one chakravartin lay dying, he received news that he would receive the ultimate accolade and be allowed to sign his name on this golden mountain. He was so excited that he decreed that his whole court would accompany him and witness the grandest honor any human being could attain. They felt so blessed and honored that upon his death, they promptly killed themselves so they might reach Heaven at the same time as their leader.

But when they arrived at the pearly gates, the gate-keeper stopped them. He said to the chakravartin, "You should go and do this alone."

"But wait a minute," the chakravartin said, infuriated. "All of these people have killed themselves in order to witness one of the greatest moments of my life."

The queen, generals, wise counselors, and ministers who gathered around him all agreed.

But the gatekeeper insisted and said, "Forgive me. I do not mean to be disrespectful, but I have been here for thousands of years. Before that, my father was here for thousands of years, and before that, his father and his father. My ancestors have been here since the beginning of time, and we have never allowed a chakravartin to go to the mountain with anyone else. They must go alone."

"That is unheard of," the chakravartin exclaimed. "These people sacrificed their lives for me. Surely you can make an exception."

"Do you think that you are the first one to come with a whole army?" the gatekeeper asked. "Very few come alone."

"And you speak to them all this way?"

"You are new, and you do not know that you will regret it if you take these people with you. All those who have come and gone have all thanked me in the end. They thanked me for making them go alone."

The chakravartin gave this a great deal of thought. All those who came before him were just as powerful and cunning as himself. He couldn't imagine why this gatekeeper

would warn him so intently if there wasn't some truth to
what he was saying. After much deliberation, he decided he
should go alone. After all, if nothing was wrong, he could always return and have his army follow him later. He received
the instructions from the gatekeeper, and entered alone.
When he reached the mountain he could hardly believe his
eyes. It was so beautiful, so expansive, beyond anything he'd
ever seen before. The mountain made the largest mountain
on earth look like a tiny toy.

But as he moved closer, he was shocked. There was
no space to sign his name. The whole mountain was filled
with name after name of all those who had come before
him. Of course, it made sense, he thought, as the mountain had been there for all eternity. Billions of chakravartins
had died. And here he thought he was so special when
he couldn't even find a tiny corner to etch his name upon.
He searched high and low, and there was no space available. What was he supposed to do now?

Finally, he had an idea. He would find the gatekeeper.
He had been here for thousands of years, and all of his rela-
tives before him. Surely he would know where the chakravartin could find room to put his name.

The gatekeeper said, "Don't waste your time. Even if
you search for a millennium, you will not find any empty
space. The mountain is filled. It has been this way forever.
The only way that you can write your name on the mountain is if you erase somebody else's and sign your name in
its place. You can forget all about being special. It is a vast

existence. That is why I tried to stop you from bringing all those people with you. You would have lost all pride, for all you can do is take someone else's name away."

The chakravartin was stunned. It was true, all of his joy dissipated. Someday, someone else would come along and erase his name. The gatekeeper agreed. "We cannot create more of the mountain; it is what it is. All the gold in Heaven has been used to create this one. You go sign and go back to the gate with your head held high. Nobody is going to know you erased someone else's name. Return, tell them that the mountain was empty, and you signed your name upon it."

But the chakravartin could not do this. He could not erase another man's name. True to his word, the chakravartin spread the message that one should not waste their life in conquering the world. One should not ask to be special, because existence does not accept anybody as special or superior…or inferior, for that matter.

Fear comes to us when we try to be somebody, but doing so won't change the situation. The only way the fear can be transcended is when we stop trying to put energy into being someone else, and put all of our energy into being ourselves. When you try to be someone else, you move further and further away from yourself. The further you go from being yourself, the further you go from knowing the truth. You are immortal; there is no death. Before searching anywhere else for what you want, search within.

The more you are willing to trust your inner self, the more you will live in the light. Everyone around you will benefit from your energy and begin to trust that they too can be more of who they really are. So before anything else, go within. Just a glimpse of your own immortality will awaken you from a nightmare. And when you do open your eyes, you will breathe in fresh, clean air laden with the fragrance of flowers showering down on you from eternity.

Who Do You Want to Be?

Here is one last story (I promise), this one about a prince who had a crooked back. Because he was a proud prince, his crooked back caused him a great deal of mental suffering. One day, he called before him the most skillful sculptor in his kingdom and asked him to make a noble statue of himself, true to his likeness in every detail, except that he would like the statue to have a straight back. The prince wished to see himself as he might have been.

For months the sculptor worked on the marble, chipping it carefully into the prince's likeness. When at last the work was done and he informed the prince of his accomplishment, great discussion ensued as to where the statue should be set up. One of the courtiers suggested they place the statue where all could see it, by the main gate. But the prince smiled sadly and shook his head. He asked that it be placed in a secret nook in the palace garden where only the prince himself could admire it.

The statue was placed as the prince ordered and promptly forgotten by everyone else. But every morning, noon, and evening, the prince quietly stole away to where it stood and looked long upon it, noting the straight back, the uplifted head, and the noble brow. And each time he gazed, something seemed to go out of the statue and into him, tingling in his blood and throbbing in his heart.

The days passed into months, and months into years, when a strange rumor began to spread throughout the land. People were speaking of the prince's back. One said it no longer looked crooked. Others said the prince seemed nobler looking. Still others said that their prince had the high look of a mighty and powerful man.

These rumors came back to the prince, and he listened with a queer smile. Then he went back into the garden to where the statue stood, and, behold, it was just as the people said. His back had become as straight as the statue's, his head had the same noble bearing; he was, in fact, the noble man his statue proclaimed him to be.

Is this just a novel idea? Not at all! Over two thousand years ago in the golden age of Athens, it was said that Grecian mothers surrounded themselves with beautiful statues so they might bring forth children that possessed the same qualities as the statues they kept close to their hearts.

Months from now, you will have an entirely new body—inside and out. Few of the cells and little of the tissue that is now in you will be there. You can be whoever you want to be.

EXERCISES

....

Meditation: Visualizing the New You

When we look in the mirror, what we see is usually not who we really are. Try this experiment: Don't look in the mirror for twenty-four hours. You'll be surprised by how differently you see yourself when you do. More often than not, our vision of ourselves is preprogrammed. In essence, we've trained our mind to see what we think we want to see, or worse, see what other people perceive us to be.

Just because others express opinions about us does not make them right. So often we use what they say to model ourselves, which is a terrible disservice to the real us who is clawing to come out. But we do it over and over again. How do I look? Did I do a good job? What should I do about this? What you do think about that? We beg for validation and confirmation from outside sources to approve of who and what we are. And let's be honest here, everyone who tells us anything is doing so from a perspective they have developed over their own lifetime. Even if it's true for them, it doesn't make it particularly functional or even healthy for you.

So here we are, looking to others to be our mirror, to reinforce our confidence, to know what we are and what we are about, what we should do and even how to do it, not realizing that they don't have a clue who they are, what they are doing, or even how to gauge themselves any better than we do.

This meditation is designed to get you off the hook. You don't have to care at all what anyone else thinks, says, or does. You need only to look inside from whatever perspective you want and you decide who you are.

Go into a deep meditation. Now imagine yourself as you would like to be. Allow the universe to repair who you used to be and heal your soul so that you may begin again. See yourself as a completely new you, the person you always wished you could be. Imagine you are smart, funny, happy, brilliant, elegant, whatever you wish to be. Replace your weaknesses with strengths, your faults with convictions. Outshine who you used to be with who you will be. Let every potential possibility you have envisioned for yourself rise up in your spirit and flow through your veins. Give birth and breathe life into your new self.

You have everything you have ever desired and are living the life you truly want to live. Visualize it with as much detail as you possibly can. You have everything you want and need in your life. Your career is right on track, your relationships are moving forward in a positive way. You are energetic and creative. You have achieved a level of success in your own life that makes you feel powerful and strong.

Now ask yourself this: Who are you in this picture? Chances are the person you want to become is acting differently than you are now. She likely is not looking at life the way you are now. Perhaps she is even dressing differently, making different decisions and choices. You don't have to wait to be that person. She exists already. All you have to do is breathe that person into life. Allow her to emerge from within you. In other words, she is not something that will come to you; she exists already. You just have to step into her being.

Journaling: Re-Scripting Your Life

Most of us are what I call action addicts. We see a condition we don't like and immediately start trying to bang things into place to fix it. The trouble is, we can't fix anything out there. We have to fix things internally first. Forcing a change with disconnected energy accomplishes nothing except for making more of a mess. Still we keep whacking away, because that's how we've been trained. Then we wonder why nothing works, why we're so tired, or why we're still stuck in the same situation.

Struggling is bad, but putting effort into something is good. Pounding away at a problem will get you nowhere. So stop fighting yourself, and get centered and quiet instead. Everything we do is infused with the energy with which we do it. If you feel frantic, everything you manifest will be disjointed. If you feel calm, everything you manifest will serve you in one way or another.

Before you embark on any new venture, pave the way with the energy. Move into the feeling place of what you would like to manifest, and flow your emotions into it first. The universe will organize the details of exactly how this will be accomplished; you need not worry about that. Your job is to create the outcome with your energy and stay out of the universe's way.

The only reason we want things is because of how they'll make us feel. Thoughts are electric, and feelings are magnetic. And since it's feeling that attracts what we desire, all we have to do is find a way to actualize that feeling and maintain it until what you want comes into your life. There are several ways to push us into that feeling place, such as creative visualization, or creating a vision board. One of the easiest is what I call "scripting." It's the same idea as visualization, but because you are actually becoming the writer, set designer, head of casting, and director, you move energy into it much more efficiently. Basically, you will end up creating a vortex for you to move into the life you want to live.

You can write your movie on paper, you can imagine it in your mind, but whatever you do, you must make it as real as possible. If we look at something as already accomplished, we make the vortex bigger. Things begin to happen. Your intuition will start to give you ideas of how to do it, have it, and be it. When someone says they were in the right place at the right time, this is how they accomplished that, whether they realized it or not. And we are scripting our lives all the time, constantly adding new characters, scenes, and scenery.

The more emotion you put into your story, the more you make it real. You should see it, taste it, smell it, touch it and, most importantly, feel it. Once you get that initial energy center formed with all the people, places, and things you desire, particularize it to give it form.

Listen patiently for the inspired ideas once you've scripted a certain scenario. Watch for unusual happenings and synchronicities around you. Perhaps you get a sudden idea to go somewhere, do something, or call someone. If the thought is accompanied with a rush of excitement, it's inspired. Do it. If it feels heavy or hard, don't bother. You ego is getting involved.

You can write a new script for any situation you want in your life. It could be an important meeting, or when you are going into a new relationship, having a baby, buying a house, or taking a trip. You can write a script for any and all of these situations. The exact situation doesn't matter so long as you're feeling good when you're thinking about it, because it will eventually happen. And the more excited you become, the more tuned in and sooner it will happen. It's like creating a tornado of magnetic energy. Before you know it, you'll be living it. The only way you won't is if you sabotage it with doubt.

Learn to script and your life will never be the same; you will become the executive producer, hired directly by the source of the big screen.

Spiritual Practice:
Throw Yourself a Going-Away Party

It's time to dress yourself up and take yourself out. There's only one condition: You must dress as you would if you were already who you want to become. If you're not sure what that would be, pick a person who emulates what you want to become, and find pictures of how that person looks and dresses. I remember a guy in high school everyone called a geek. He was seventeen and dressed like he was forty. He always wore a button-down shirt and carried a leather briefcase. He looked so out of place, it wasn't even funny. But that's just who he was. And guess what? He grew up to be the CEO of a major investment firm. He started dressing the part early and it certainly paid off, whether he knew it at the time or not.

Take time to meditate on who you would like to be. Then use props, accents, words, behavior, and clothing to try it out and see how it feels for one entire day. It will show you that shifting is possible, even if it's temporary. By stepping outside of your habitual identity and self-image, you will be teaching your subconscious mind that you *can* become exactly who you'd like to be.

Nine

Total Transitions

We create suffering for ourselves and for others through our attachment to the notion of "I." But, spiritually, there is no such thing as "I." It is an illusory manifestation of our basic will and desire to exist as a separate entity. In short, it really is the ego. By believing in the reality of an "I," we suffer the delusion that we are in fact separate from everybody else and get fully engrossed by our own needs.

But we cannot run a world full of over seven billion people based upon the premise that everyone is responsible for him or herself. Though many of us wish things were different, we tend to continue on this fatalist course because this is the way everyone else is acting, and no one wants to be left out. We assume that if everyone else is out for themselves, we should be too. We then turn away from helping others with arguments like, "I can't change the world. Why should I even bother? I know I can't make a difference."

The world of the ego is a world of ups and downs, darkness and light. Heaven is a realm of constant peace that transcends the complexities of duality and change. We choose the world we live in and can easily shift our perspective to the one where infinite potential abounds. If we die in the world of the ego, we are reborn into one where the spirit knows no limits and the possibilities are endless.

We are all sacred beings. It is only our perspective that distorts our sense of the sacred within others and ourselves. We all come from the same divine source and are created in its image. Our origins are one and the same. If this is true, then all of us are equal in every sense of the word. And if we are all divinely sanctioned, we can be nothing but sacred by virtue of just existing.

Since we are all holy, it stands to reason that we have the ineffaceable right to be exactly who we are and create a life that is happy, healthy, and whole. So what are you waiting for? Stop pretending you are anything less than perfect, and get on with living a joyous, prosperous, abundant life. The trouble is, most of us understand this, but we don't believe it on a pragmatic level.

All we have to do to find that place within us is relax into our experiences and remember that it is all perfection. Our inner guidance is the only thing that will forever keep us on the track to truth. These eternal truths then become our compass during times of rapid transition, binding us emotionally to a steady and firm course. Love is the only absolute reality; it never changes or dies. Dwelling in that which does not change while everything around us is changing all the time is our key to inner peace.

How to Eat an Elephant

I was born in Pakistan, so it wasn't uncommon for my father to ask me things such as "How do you eat an elephant?"

I remembered this because years ago I was worried about something that I thought was life-or-death. My world could have conceivably crumbled. I was in tears at the time, and all my father could say was, "How do you eat an elephant?"

My background is somewhat illusive to me and it threw me into a world that was both simultaneously real and unreal. For a minute there, I actually wondered if he had eaten an elephant. And if he did, how he did it and why he did it. The puzzled look on my face must have clued him in. He started laughing and said, "There's only one way to eat an elephant, and that's one bite at a time."

Change will come in varying degrees. We get frustrated when we look at the whole picture instead of dealing with one aspect at a time. Absolutely everything can be broken down into smaller, more manageable steps. As they say, a journey of a thousand miles begins with a single step; we can only eat an elephant one bite at a time.

If we break things down, the immensity of the situation softens, and before we know it, we have surmounted the entire situation. Simplicities are our lifelines in any set of circumstances; they help us remember that things are not so overwhelming, and you probably will not feel so anxious if you remember this. I have found that when you take small steps toward what your intuition is indicating, new doors begin to open. For instance, when I knew I had to move, I was completely overwhelmed. I didn't know where I was going to move to, and the idea of packing up an entire house wasn't something I was looking forward to. I was exhausted just thinking about it. I asked the universe for a sign of acknowledgement, or a sign of anything for that matter. That afternoon a friend of mine randomly told me about how her neighbors just moved in. I asked if there were any boxes left over and, if so, if they wouldn't mind if I used them. My friend ended up bringing me over forty boxes that night. She also orchestrated a packing party. This is the universe's way of saying I was on the right track and to just keep going. Within a week, I had a place to move to.

Your inner guidance will always direct you in loving and compassionate ways. What we don't often realize is that all change comes from within. It is not something that happens to us. It is something that on some level we require for the expansion of our soul's experience.

What the Shift Happened?

Most of us have heard of the hundredth-monkey syndrome. Just in case you haven't, it was a unique phenomenon that occurred the 1950s when a group of Japanese scientists provided wild monkeys with sweet potatoes dropped in the sand in order to study their behavior. Although they seemed to like this new delicacy, they found the dirt unpleasant. One day, they noticed one monkey do something that was rather extraordinary. Imo, as she was named, solved the problem by washing the potato before eating it. Suddenly, she started doing this on a regular basis, always washing the potato before consuming it. Pretty soon, some of the other monkeys who had observed her started doing the same thing.

So far, that's not such a big deal. But what was interesting is that scientists observing monkeys on other islands began exhibiting the same behavior. There was no connection between the islands, none whatsoever. No monkey booked a trip to one island or another. There's absolutely no explanation for this behavior, except to say that washing potatoes was a new level of consciousness for these monkeys. And once enough of them accepted the idea, it was apparently transferred to the monkeys on surrounding islands without any physical contact or direct communication. It is my belief that this is how a shift in consciousness works, whether you're a monkey or not.

Every individual's consciousness is connected to, and is a part of, the collective consciousness. When a small group of individuals have moved into a new level of awareness and significantly changed their behavior, other individuals will follow.

When we look at the world around us it's easy to feel overwhelmed and helpless in how we can have any effect whatsoever. The world seems too big, with so many problems, that we cannot fathom how one person can possibly make a positive change. But you can. One individual, just like one monkey, can transform their world, and then when they do those around them will follow.

The world is a mirror, and it can only reflect to us that which we are. So when you change, the world around you changes. It's not the other way around. If you intuitively trace what you have gone through in this book—learning to trust yourself and take care of yourself by gradually releasing old habits and patterns—you should notice that your friends, family, and associates all seem to be feeling and acting differently as well. As your own drama disappears, those around you will feel lighter as well.

The shift in your consciousness has created a new reality. To whatever degree you experienced the presence of the universe in your own body, the less you feel afraid. You opened yourself up to more power, fears got flushed to the surface and released, and a solid base of trust was established within you. Others feel this and in it will find the support to open up to more of their own power and truth. The people and things around you reflect who you are in increasingly positive ways. The more light you allow within you, the brighter the world you live in will be.

Visualization and affirmations are good things, but without action they are nothing more than delusional. If the world truly is our mirror, we have to keep working upon our own inner world. We have to recognize and affirm that as we sincerely do our own inner work, the world is also being transformed. With all the pain, violence, poverty, and chaos out there, all we can do is change what lies within ourselves if we want to see it change on the outside.

Be open to any inner guidance you may receive to seek support in your healing process through a counselor or therapist, friends, a workshop or group, or any other form. On a daily basis, visualize your life and the world as you would like to see them.

Finally, ask your inner guidance to let you know clearly if there is any specific action you need to take toward your own or the world's healing. Then continue to trust and follow your intuition, knowing that you will be led to do whatever is necessary. You are a spiritual being made in God's image and likeness, and all you have to do in this moment is ask the universe to reflect back to you that greatness that is already within you.

The power of the universe is healing and transforming you. As you are healed and transformed, so is the whole world healed and transformed.

Unconditional Love

We can only love one another unconditionally when we remember that we are all touchingly alike. With our intuition, we realize our separateness may be more perception than actuality. When we go deep within, we catch glimpses of a truer reality in which we all share our deepest longings.

It is love that teaches us how to live life. Our inner guidance moves us through relationships romantic and otherwise which teach us how to navigate life's ups and downs. It is a lesson in learning to love without expecting results, rewards, or payment of any kind. This is the only way to love, letting ourselves grow and change and embracing others as they do the same. We can be ourselves and let everyone around us be exactly who they are.

Living the Life of Your Dreams

We are only here for a set number of years, days, or possibly hours. (It has to be more than minutes, because I have to finish writing this!) We make what we hope are wise choices and do the best we can. For the most part, that's all we can do. But we can also dive into the river of wisdom and guidance that flows through and around us as often as we can. If we choose to tap into its rich depths for insight and discover the heart of who we are, we will always be living life to the best of our ability.

A New World

From where I am sitting, I can see the ocean. The sun is setting and ribbons of burnt orange and blood red blaze across the water. The waves ebb and flow, hugging the sandy shore and throwing bubbly kisses at the rocks. I love the ocean. It reminds me that nothing remains the same. Sometimes it is bright and shining, with the promise of a new day on the horizon. And, sometimes it is misty and cloudy, shrouded with a mysterious veil, concealing another world.

In my meditative state, I contemplate what lies beneath the waves, wondering what other civilizations are now buried beneath the watery surface. I am certain there must have been an ancient land that flourished and thrived. What happened to a place that was once so glorious and magnificent that it could crumble and disintegrate over time? On a grander level, it is no different than what we experience in our own lives; loss and gain, and the gift that emerges from the alchemy of change itself.

Even though the ocean washed away the rubble, something magical remained. The ground deep down below shimmers with a blinding luminosity that will light the world once again. I know now that this world never existed somewhere out there, but deep within our own souls.

It is my new world. It is your new world. It is our new world.

EXERCISES

....

Meditation: You Are the Light of the Universe
Get comfortable and close your eyes. Breathe deeply and mindfully, and drop into a deep, quiet place within. Focus on your breath and relaxing every part of your body. Now surround yourself with white light. The white light symbolizes purity and will help rid you of any negativity. Feel this light moving down through your crown chakra at the

top of your head into your body. Breathe deeply as all of the negativity in you is replaced by this white light. Visualize the light moving down through your entire body; your arms, chest, and legs and feet.

Take several more breaths and relax your mind. Remind yourself that you are a divine being. Don't fight it. Take your mind off of any imperfections that make you feel as if this may not be true. Instead, look deeper within and you will know being divine is part of your natural heritage. Breathe the white light into every area of your body, into every cell in your body until you feel full and complete. Let the light permeate your being. Ask that this light of the universe release and heal all the darkness of fear and limitation within you. Ask for the light of the universe to uncover the darkness of ignorance, fear, and limitation within you and in the world. Imagine that your body is glowing and radiating with the light. Your body and your mind are being transformed, reminding you of the whole and perfect child of the universe that you are. Nothing or no one can take that away from you. You are perfect exactly the way you are, including with every mistake you've made and every idiosyncrasy you have. There is no limit to what you can achieve or become.

Understanding that you are pure love is all that matters in the end. Learning to feel it, know it, and be it. To act on that and not react is the only lesson there is to learn. When you can do this, you know you are beautiful, precious, and magnificent. You own that already because you are the spectacular divinity that you are.

Stay in the meditation as long as you can, allowing yourself to fully embrace the new person you have become. Feel the light and laughter and love within you. When you feel completely renewed, surround yourself with angels before you return to reality.

You are the light of the world, and with the angels by your side, you may not make miracles happen, but you will be the miracle you wished to create. From this place of sheer joy and bliss, imagine that the world is a mirror of your own transformation. Imagine that as you are healed, the world is healed as well. When ready, bring yourself back feeling completely joyful and free.

Journaling: Remembering Your Purpose

I remember reading this quote by Joseph Campbell from *The Power of Myth*: "I say, follow your bliss and don't be afraid, and doors will open where you didn't know they were going to be."

Follow my bliss? He made it sound so easy. But what was my bliss? I tried and tried to figure it out. Finally, I was just blissed out! Here are some questions I used to help me along my way. Answer honestly. Answer spontaneously. There are no wrong answers, so simply write what comes to you from the heart. This is not a test, so have fun.

- If you had a million dollars, what would you do with it?

- What have you always wished that you could do that you haven't done?

- What have you always wished you could be that you haven't been?

- If you could change one thing about yourself, what would it be?

- If you could change one thing about the world, what would it be?

- What person, dead or alive, would you most like to emulate and why?

- How would you describe your ideal life?

If these questions aren't helping, make up your own. Play around. Choose ones that force you to examine your purpose in life. Here are a few more examples, just to get you going:

- What have you always wished you could do?

- What would you like your life's work to be?

- Where do you want to be spiritually?

- What kind of person would you like to become?

You get the idea. Don't get too wrapped up in what it would mean if you achieve your goal, i.e., is it really possible that I could get there? Don't make it a big deal, but easy and fun. Once you set the goal, it means you have set a sight on a specific destination. You still have to get there, which is most of the fun.

A goal is a desire, target, aim, hope, dream, purpose, ambition, aspiration, or objective. The more intense the desire, the more important the goal, and more likely you will be motivated to do whatever it takes to achieve it. Human beings are goal-setters by nature. Everyone has goals whether they know it or not. Getting up in the morning, going to work, cleaning the house, cooking dinner—whatever you desire to do is a goal. Whenever you want to get from where you are to somewhere else, whether it's getting out of bed and going to the store or changing a career, you set a goal.

Are you still at a loss? Everyone has value as a person and as a resource for others. You have talents, skills, and experience that can be turned into service for others. List your expertise, talents, and skills. (List everything. Don't hold back. If you have a talent for cleaning house, say so.) What games did you enjoy playing and excel at a child? What talents do you have that people will pay for? What are you best talents? What knowledge do you have that others could benefit from? What talents do you have that could be expanded upon or bettered in some way?

Dig deep. You may have done volunteer work that companies would pay a lot of money for. Perhaps in college you participated in activities that demanded skills you mastered. Search into your memory bank, and write down anything you can think of. It could be something you did years ago that seems insignificant, but it may have been a valuable experience or part of your résumé, skills, talents, and education. This could be a golden treasure.

If you feel you still don't have a handle on your life purpose, there is one more journaling exercise I would like you to try. Lock yourself in a room by yourself. Light candles, burn incense, and do whatever you need to do to become relaxed and comfortable.

When you are ready, turn the page and begin writing. It doesn't matter what you write, just write. Don't try to analyze it, figure it out, or even make sense of it. For God's sake, please don't try to make it logical. Simply write…and keep writing. When do you stop? When do you know you've found the answer? Simple: when you start to cry. Yup, that's it. When you have written something that brings a tear to your eye, you will know you are finished.

But what if you didn't start crying, you wonder? Get more paper, because you didn't write long enough or hard enough! This could take ten minutes or ten hours. How long it will take you is strictly personal.

Begin and find out. You'll be glad you did.

Spiritual Practice: Love Something Today

Life in transition is a grand adventure. What I learned in the end was that the meaning in my life was my life. If you seize the vastness of the moment, you will naturally develop unconditional love and compassion, not so much for others, but for yourself. You'll have a deeper appreciation and reverence for life, and you will have become more passionate and patient, having realized that you no longer have to wait for a better job, a newer car, the perfect relationship, or anything else in the material world to show up in order to make you happy. Your suffering becomes more about what you found and than what you lost, and you can live a joyful life now because you chose to do so. When you do you will find that your pain can only lead you back to love.

There are many paths that lead to the fulfillment of your dreams, and no two paths will ever be alike. But the right path for you will always be focused on love. Finding love within our own selves is what we came here to learn. When we can look into the world and feel love, even if it's a tiny piece of love within the experience at the time, you have become a Master. Our lives will take on the rhythm of the universe's dance and move in phenomenally beautiful ways. We will automatically find abundance, health, and happiness.

Yes, it takes a bit of an effort, but try to love something in every moment of every day. Marvel at something. Feel the joy of what is before you rather than the pain of what is behind you. Appreciate, love, laugh, be silly, be funny, and be joyful. When you are having fun, your divine intuition will find and guide you by keeping you connected to your core. And when we are tuned in to the essence of our being, we naturally attract the people, places, and things we want into our lives. We start by sending out love only to receive it in return.

Here are a few fun ways to get you started:

- Tell the bug that's buzzing over your head right now that you really love and appreciate it.

- Feel the true wonder of a flower.

- Manufacture delight over absolutely nothing.

- Sing a love song to a tree.

- Kiss the hamburger before you eat it.

- Kiss yourself after you do.

- Transmit a deep appreciation toward the sun.

- Tell your car how much in love you are with everyone and everything.

- Love yourself as you walk out the door every day.

In Conclusion:
Howling in the Wind

Late one night, I heard the howling of a coyote in the distance. It was a primitive sound, eerie and wild. A cold sound on a cold winter's night. The wailing cries made the hair on the back of my neck stand on end, and they stirred something deep within the center of my being, bringing to mind an old Native American Indian legend about Coyote and starlight. A Navajo Indian recounted a story to a woman as she looked up at the stars. It went something like this:

———

Long ago, before man walked upon the earth, there were no stars to be found in the night sky. The animals gathered in the darkness and decided it might be nice to have something other than the moon, which was somewhat unreliable, shed some light upon them so that they might hunt at night. Together they went to the Great Spirit and asked for help. The Great Spirit agreed that this was indeed a splendid idea. Immediately, he grabbed a shining stone from the river and tossed it into the night sky, where it became a shining star. "Wow," the animals thought. "We have light!"

They asked Great Spirit if they might be able to do the same. "Of course," the Great Spirit said. In fact, he informed them that this could be an extraordinary way for them to see themselves. They could toss many shining stones into the night sky and create pictures of their own likenesses. The animals were very excited and couldn't wait to begin. All night, they tossed shining stones into the sky, drawing outlines of their own beings. All of them did this except Coyote, who couldn't understand why these depraved animals would play such a silly game. "Surely, they will grow tired and still not have much light," he thought before returning to the business of sleeping the night away.

Sure enough, the animals grew tired and had not completed their images as the first light of day began caressing the sky. In desperation, they went to Coyote and asked if he could help, since surely he would have plenty of energy. Coyote contemplated the idea and decided he would finish the drawings and then create the biggest, brightest image of all, his own. He collected all of the stones that the animals gathered and tossed them carelessly into the night sky, wildly scattering them about. The sky was filled with bright stars, but none of them completed a clear picture. In his haste, Coyote realized he had no stones and no time left to create his own magnificent image.

Coyote howled into the night, furious at the loss of his own grand heavenly design that would have been displayed for all eternity. And from that day forward, the sound of coyotes' mournful wails emanated from a primal longing woven deep within their souls.

————

Scientists will tell you that it is a coyote's nature to howl. The cries regather the pack so they might feel safe and secure. I believe that as humans, we all have the same longing—to be called back to the spirit that underlies our very existence.

The winds of change will blow, carrying the scent of something that is not quite right in our lives. In these moments our soul often urges us to move, to change, and find a different path. We can almost feel the ground beneath our feet shift.

When we become alert to this, the sound of our souls howling at the moon and the insistent sense of longing for something lost, we're forced to stop, be quiet, listen deeply, and become attentive to our primal needs. Upon awakening, we search for wholeness and completeness.

Go inside and ask your inner guidance system where the silver cord is. It cannot be broken, only lost. When you find it, you will know. The cord will anchor you among the waves that toss you about the stormy sea you call life. Peace will flow through you, and calmness shall still your restless heart. Then with every step you take, the path will appear beneath your feet, guiding you to exactly where you are meant to be.

Recommended Reading

Copeland-Payton, Nancy. *The Losses of Our Lives: The Sacred Gifts of Renewal in Everyday Loss.* Woodstock, VT: Skylight Paths Publishing, 2011.

Das, Surya (Lama). *Letting Go of the Person You Used to Be: Lessons on Change, Loss, and Spiritual Transformation.* New York: Broadway Books, 2003.

Deits, Bob. *Life After Loss: A Practical Guide to Renewing Your Life After Experiencing Major Loss.* Boston: Lifelong Books, 2009.

Finley, Guy. *The Secret of Letting Go.* Woodbury, MN: Llewellyn Publications, 2007.

Kübler-Ross, Elisabeth, and David Kessler. *On Grief and Grieving: Finding the Meaning of Grief Through the Five Stages of Loss.* New York: Scribner, 2007.

Kumar, Sameet M., PhD. *Grieving Mindfully: A Compassionate and Spiritual Guide to Coping with Loss.* Oakland, CA: New Harbinger Publications, 2005.

May, Gerald G. *The Dark Night of the Soul: A Psychiatrist Explores the Connection Between Darkness and Spiritual Growth.* San Francisco: HarperSanFrancisco, 2005.

Rando, Therese A. *How to Go On Living When Someone You Love Dies.* New York: Bantam, 1991.

Taylor, Terry. *A Spirituality for Brokenness: Discovering Your Deepest Self in Difficult Times.* Woodstock, VT: SkyLight Paths, 2009.

Williamson, Marianne. *The Gift of Change: Spiritual Guidance for a Radically New Life.* San Francisco: HarperSanFrancisco, 2004.

Bibliography

Beattie, Melody. *The Language of Letting Go*. Center City, Minnesota: Hazelden, 1990.

Bloomfield, Harold, Melba Colgrove, and Peter McWilliams. *How to Survive the Loss of a Love*. Algonac, MI: Mary Books/Prelude Press, 2000.

Borysenko, Joan. *Woman's Journey to God: Finding the Feminine Path*. New York: Riverhead Books, 2000.

Copeland-Payton, Nancy. *The Losses of Our Lives, The Sacred Gifts of Renewal in Everyday Loss*. Woodstock, VT: Skylight Paths Publishing, 2011.

Das, Surya (Lama). *Letting Go of the Person You Used to Be: Lessons on Change, Loss, and Spiritual Transformation.* New York: Broadway Books, 2003.

Emerson, Ralph Waldo. *Self-Reliance and Other Essays.* Mineola, NY: Dover Publications, 1993.

Frankl, V. E. *Man's Search for Meaning.* New York: Pocket Books, 2007.

Gawain, Shakti (with Laurel King). *Living in the Light: A Guide to Personal and Planetary Transformation.* New York: Bantam Books, 1986.

Hanh, Thich Nhat. *The Heart of the Buddha's Teaching: Transforming Suffering Into Peace, Joy, and Liberation.* New York: Broadway Books, 1999.

Holmes, Ernest. *The Science of Mind: The Complete Edition* (reprint). New York: Tarcher, 2010.

Keyes, Ken, Jr. *The Hundreth Monkey.* Camarillo, CA: DeVorss & Co, 1984.

Kraus, Donald. *The Book of Job, Annotated & Explained.* Woodstock, VT: Skylight Paths Publishing, 2012.

Kumar, Sameet M. *Grieving Mindfully: A Compassionate and Spiritual Guide to Coping with Loss.* Oakland, CA: New Harbinger Publications, 2005.

Kushner, Harold. *When Bad Things Happen to Good People*. New York: Anchor, 2004.

Osho, Osho International Foundation. *Fear: Understanding and Accepting the Insecurities of Life*. New York: St. Martin's Press, 2012.

Robinson, Lynn A. *Divine Intuition: Your Guide to Creating a Life You Love*. New York: Dorling Kindersley, 2001.

Shakespeare, William. *The Complete Works of William Shakespeare* (Leather classic edition). New York: Barnes & Noble, 1994.

Williamson, Marianne. *The Gift of Change: Spiritual Guidance for a Radically New Life*. San Francisco: HarperSanFrancisco, 2004.

Yogananda, Paramahansa. *Autobiography of a Yogi* (edition unknown). Los Angeles: Self-Realization Fellowship, 1998.

GET MORE AT LLEWELLYN.COM

Visit us online to browse hundreds of our books and decks, plus sign up to receive our e-newsletters and exclusive online offers.

- Free tarot readings • Spell-a-Day • Moon phases
- Recipes, spells, and tips • Blogs • Encyclopedia
- Author interviews, articles, and upcoming events

GET SOCIAL WITH LLEWELLYN

Find us on Facebook

www.Facebook.com/LlewellynBooks

Follow us on

www.Twitter.com/Llewellynbooks

GET BOOKS AT LLEWELLYN

LLEWELLYN ORDERING INFORMATION

Order online: Visit our website at www.llewellyn.com to select your books and place an order on our secure server.

Order by phone:
- Call toll free within the U.S. at 1-877-NEW-WRLD (1-877-639-9753)
- Call toll free within Canada at 1-866-NEW-WRLD (1-866-639-9753)
- We accept VISA, MasterCard, and American Express

Order by mail:
Send the full price of your order (MN residents add 6.875% sales tax) in U.S. funds, plus postage and handling to: Llewellyn Worldwide, 2143 Wooddale Drive, Woodbury, MN 55125-2989

POSTAGE AND HANDLING:

STANDARD: (U.S. & Canada)
(Please allow 12 business days)
$25.00 and under, add $4.00.
$25.01 and over, FREE SHIPPING.

INTERNATIONAL ORDERS (airmail only):
$16.00 for one book, plus $3.00 for each additional book.

Visit us online for more shipping options. Prices subject to change.

FREE CATALOG!

To order, call
1-877-
NEW-WRLD
ext. 8236
or visit our
website

FINDING YOUR OWN PATH
TO LASTING LOVE

the
INTUITIVE HEART
OF
ROMANCE

SERVET HASAN

The Intuitive Heart of Romance
Finding Your Own Path to Lasting Love
SERVET HASAN

Relationships are drastically changing. Women have more choices than ever when it comes to careers, marriage, kids, and love. Given these new possibilities, how can women create healthy, lasting relationships? The answer is profoundly spiritual.

Servet Hasan offers fresh, practical advice in this spiritual guide to the evolving world of love and relationships. Soul-centered meditations and exercises help women to access and develop their innate intuitive gifts to strengthen and deepen romantic relationships.

As they learn to use their intuition, women will gain insight into commitment, sacred sex, relinquishing fears, resolving conflicts, moving beyond dead-end relationships, releasing repressed beliefs, and creating a deeply spiritual bond with their partners.

978-0-7387-2584-0, 288 pp., 5³⁄₁₆ x 8   **$15.95**

Love and Intuition
A Psychic's Guide to Creating Lasting Love
SHERRIE DILLARD

Love, by its very nature, is profoundly spiritual. Each of us can harness this transformative emotion by embracing our own natural intuition.

Building on the success of *Discover Your Psychic Type*, professional psychic Sherrie Dillard presents a life-changing paradigm based on the four love types. This unique book teaches you to develop your intuition to attract and sustain love, while enriching your relationship with your spouse or partner, friends, and yourself.

Once you find out your intuitive love type—emotional, spiritual, mental, or physical—you can then determine your spouse or partner's love type, and learn practical ways to strengthen your relationship and heighten intimacy.

978-0-7387-1555-1, 336 pp., 6 x 9   **$16.95**

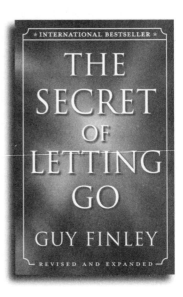

The Secret of Letting Go
Guy Finley

Llewellyn is proud to present the revised and expanded edition of our best-selling self-help book, *The Secret of Letting Go*. With more than 200,000 copies sold, Guy Finley's message of self-liberation has touched people around the world. Discover how to extinguish self-defeating thoughts and habits that undermine true happiness. Exploring relationships, depression, and stress, his inspiring words can help you let go of debilitating anxiety, unnecessary anger, paralyzing guilt, and painful heartache. True stories, revealing dialogues, and thought-provoking questions will guide you toward the endless source of inner strength and emotional freedom that resides within us all.

978-0-7387-1198-0, 312 pp., 5³⁄₁₆ x 8   **$14.95**

KATHRYN HARWIG

The

RETURN

of

INTUITION

**Awakening Psychic Gifts
in the Second Half of Life**

The Return of Intuition

Awakening Psychic Gifts in the Second Half of Life
KATHRYN HARWIG

Natural psychic sensitivity is often associated with children. However, *The Return of Intuition* reveals a little-known, widespread phenomenon of profound intuitive awakening occurring in adults—usually around the age of fifty.

Bringing this remarkable trend to light is psychic medium Kathryn Harwig, who has helped clients nationwide understand, nurture, and embrace their newfound psychic awareness. Their inspiring stories highlight what triggers this life-changing gift—usually illness or the death of a loved one—and how it can be used to aid others, receive messages from friends and family in spirit, and begin life anew with confidence, courage, and clarity. Affirming the joys of aging, this unique spiritual guide offers comfort and support to the elders of our society, encouraging them to reclaim their once-revered roles—as the crone, shaman, and sage—by passing on spiritual wisdom to a new generation.

978-0-7387-1880-4, 216 pp., 5³/₁₆ x 8 **$15.95**

Melissa Alvarez

365 Ways

to Raise Your

Frequency

SIMPLE TOOLS TO INCREASE
YOUR SPIRITUAL ENERGY
FOR BALANCE, PURPOSE, AND JOY

365 Ways to Raise Your Frequency

*Simple Tools to Increase Your Spiritual
Energy for Balance, Purpose, and Joy*
MELISSA ALVAREZ

The soul's vibrational rate, our spiritual frequency, has a huge impact on our lives. As it increases, so does our capacity to calm the mind, connect with angels and spirit guides, find joy and enlightenment, and achieve what we want in life.

This simple and inspiring guide makes it easy to elevate your spiritual frequency every day. Choose from a variety of ordinary activities, such as singing and cooking. Practice visualization exercises and techniques for reducing negativity, manifesting abundance, tapping into Universal Energy, and connecting with your higher self. Discover how generous actions and a positive attitude can make a difference. You'll also find long-term projects and guidance for boosting your spiritual energy to new heights over a lifetime.

978-0-7387-2740-0, 432 pp., 5 x 7   **$16.95**

To order, call 1-877-NEW-WRLD
Prices subject to change without notice
Order at Llewellyn.com 24 hours a day, 7 days a week!

"An expansive and comprehensive manual that will help you understand
your soul's purpose. I highly recommend this book."
—BRIAN L. WEISS, MD, author of *Many Lives, Many Masters*

SoulVisioning

Clear the Past, Create Your Future

SUSAN WISEHART

Soul Visioning
Clear the Past, Create Your Future
SUSAN WISEHART

This groundbreaking book teaches you how to create a life of passion and purpose by following your soul's wisdom. Using breakthrough methods such as Energy Psychology (acupuncture for the emotions without the needles), guided journeys, forgiveness practices, and past life and life-between-lives regression, you'll discover practical, step-by-step techniques to heal the unconscious beliefs that block the awareness of your true spiritual identity and life purpose.

The soul-visioning journey connects you with your Higher Self to guide you into the ideal expression of your soul in your work, relationships, health, finances, and spirituality. Powerful and inspiring case examples with long-term follow-up interviews demonstrate the remarkable results that Wisehart's clients have experienced from these life-changing techniques.

978-0-7387-1408-0, 336 pp., 6 x 9   **$17.95**
